Stoked!

An inspiring story about courage,
determination and the power of dreams

CHRIS BERTISH

Winner of the 2010 Mavericks Big Wave Invitational

Z ZEBRA PRESS

Published by Zebra Press
an imprint of Penguin Random House South Africa (Pty) Ltd
Company Reg. No. 1966/003153/07
The Estuaries No. 4, Oxbow Crescent, Century Avenue, Century City, Cape Town, 7441
PO Box 1144, Cape Town, 8000, South Africa
www.penguinrandomhouse.co.za

Published in 2015
Reprinted in 2015, 2016 (twice), 2017 (twice) and 2018 (twice)

9 10 8

PUBLISHER: Marlene Fryer
MANAGING EDITOR: Ronel Richter-Herbert
EDITOR: Bronwen Maynier
PROOFREADER: Ronel Richter-Herbert
COVER DESIGNER: Sean Robertson
TEXT DESIGNER: Ryan Africa
TYPESETTER: Ryan Africa/Monique van den Berg

Set in 11.5 pt on 16 pt Minion

Printed by **novus print**, a Novus Holdings company

MIX
Paper from
responsible sources
FSC
www.fsc.org   FSC® C022948

Penguin Random House is committed to a sustainable future for our business, our readers
and our planet. This book is made from Forest Stewardship Council ® certified paper.

ISBN 978 1 77022 764 4 (print)
ISBN 978 1 77022 765 1 (ePub)
ISBN 978 1 77022 766 8 (PDF)

Disclaimer

Every effort has been made to credit the correct person for the images used
in this book. Where we may have omitted a name or been unable to find the
copyright holder, we ask that the relevant party contact us in order for their
name to be included in a reprint edition of this book.

Contents

Dedicated to a legend

I would like to dedicate this book to my dad,
a true waterman, a great father, a hero, a friend and a legend.
Thank you for showing me there was always another way
and for teaching me to follow my dreams.

To all of you out there who have the courage to
follow through on your dreams, you are my heroes,
because to truly live is to live with the courage to try.

Stoked (1) Amped, excited, filled with crazy enthusiasm; pure joy, infectious energy, wild exuberance, adrenaline-fuelled, totally thrilled, naturally high on life.

(2) The feeling you get when you catch your first wave.

(3) The feeling that you just HAVE to catch one more ... and that it should be even bigger and better than the last ...

Dedication to the big-wave brotherhood

Big-wave surfers are a unique breed.
We are drawn to the big open ocean swells that come
with little warning, that call our names and lure us
to the challenge, to brave them, ride them, tame them,
to be in tune with them. We plan our lives around the ocean.
It runs our daily life, our yearly calendar.
We have to be ready, all the time. In the same way that a
firefighter waits for the call for a fire, we're on standby 24/7,
365 days a year, for those swells. We wait, we watch, we plan,
we prepare, never knowing when, where, how big or how
dangerous they will be or when they will come ... but when they
do ... we will be there waiting, waiting and ready, physically
and mentally prepared to drop everything and just go.
Some of us will travel halfway around the world and back to
find that perfect big wave. It's just who we are and how we are
hardwired. It's an obsession that can ruin lives, relationships,
jobs and anything else that tries to stand in its way.
But there is nothing else quite like it.
We are the gladiators of the deep, we are the
warriors of the sea, we are the big-wave brotherhood.

This book contains a very special "flick-book animation" by artist Chris Brehem. Flick through each page in quick succession to follow big-wave surfer Chris Bertish as he paddles into a wave, takes the drop, rides the wave and gets barrelled on his way to fulfilling his dreams of glory. Give it a try and enjoy watching Chris surf the wave of his life ...

Foreword

Chris Bertish tries to explain it this way:

Imagine that you and he were, for whatever reason, forced to face the fastest and most ferocious cricket bowler in the world. Like you, he would probably be terrified. But imagine if both of you had played cricket all your lives and had progressed to the point where you had the skills not just to face the bowler, but perhaps even, on occasion, to dispatch his deliveries to the boundary. This, he claims, explains why he is not terrified of 60-foot waves. He has been in the ocean all his life and what he does today is simply a result of all those thousands of hours of observation, wisdom and practice.

But, at least for me, this explanation does not really work. For while like many I have played cricket and even batted against quite fast schoolboy bowling without great fear, I once surfed a six-foot wave – and was immobilised by anxiety. When the surf was any bigger, I stayed on the shore. There is something about the ocean and the power of waves that transcends anything humans can do to one another on the sports field. While many play cricket and perforce must bat against ferocious fast bowling, there are very, very few who travel the world seeking to impose themselves on the largest breaking waves on our planet.

And fewer still who, as you will learn in these pages, do it in the manner of Chris Bertish.

Such men and women are very different from the rest of us. And they are different not just by way of the physical person that each has become through their practising and training, but, more importantly, because of what each has done to their minds.

I recently met Diana Nyad, who had swum for more than 50 hours in her successful completion of the 160-kilometre ocean swim from Cuba to Key West, Florida. Four times she had failed, succeeding on her fifth attempt at age 62. Sometime after the swim she participated in a research study to determine how her brain responded to a simulated life-threatening emergency. The researchers were astounded – her brain was utterly untroubled as she logically and unemotionally worked through her options in a manner they had never before observed. She exhibited what Chris told me is the first rule of big-wave surfing: When you panic, don't panic. As you will read in his book, that approach has saved Chris's life on more than one occasion. Without fear, there is no panic. But how some can train their brains not to fear a 60-foot wave is the mystery that compels us to read Chris's story. Is it possible that we could all be like Chris if we worked each day as he does on the mental and emotional sides of our being? Not just on the physical?

But, like Diana Nyad, there is another, even more compelling reason why Chris's story is so engrossing. I thought of this as I watched South African cricketer A.B. de Villiers in his single utterly unbelievable innings that has completely redefined what is possible in cricket batting. In just 44 minutes, De Villiers broke the shackles that have held the minds of cricket batters captive for more than three centuries. As I watch the grainy images of Chris Bertish surfing 60-foot waves at Mavericks or 35-foot waves at Jaws, I experience the same feeling. So tiny on the waves that he seems to sometimes disappear, I am overcome with this thought: Humans do not belong here. It is impossible for a human to survive what is about to happen. And when he does survive because of the manner in which he has prepared himself for more than three decades, we realise that our definition of what is possible is constrained only by our own fears and lack of imagination. And by our feeble choice not to push the boundaries of human achievement beyond the safety of the mundane that most of us accept as our designated life's destiny.

What is it about these men and women who do not understand why the rest of us put such unnecessary limitations on what we believe to be possible? That is the greater question that this book begins to address. I do not know the answer, but my knowledge of Chris suggests some clues.

First, these men and women are without hubris; their outstanding characteristic is humility and self-reflection. This is essential, for nature will expose any weakness. And it matters not who you think you are. When you are 30 feet below the surface, not knowing which way is up, and being dragged along at 40 kilometres an hour by a 60-foot wave that will release you only after 90 seconds, your only hope of survival is full knowledge of exactly who you really are. Believing you are something other than that is the quickest way to death.

Herb Elliott, the Australian miler who retired at age 22, the world mile record holder, Olympic gold medallist and never beaten at that distance in any race in his life, said that to break a world record, the athlete needs the arrogance to believe that he can run faster than anyone who has ever lived, and the humility to actually go out and do it. But when your life is at stake, as it is each time Chris Bertish takes off on a wave at Jaws or Mavericks, humility and self-knowledge are all that will save you.

Second, they always do what is right, whatever the personal cost.

I experienced this when I once spoke with Chris at a relatively inconsequential lecture that we gave together. Three hours before we were scheduled to speak, Chris phoned me to say that he had acute appendicitis but that he would still complete his lecture and then go for the surgery that he needed. I urged him not to be stupid – "Your health," I told him, "is more important than this lecture." He completely ignored my dire warning that he might die as a result. Instead, he spoke for one hour without once mentioning that he was in excruciating pain and without giving the slightest impression that there was anything remotely wrong with him. After his lecture he patiently answered the audience's questions before slipping away unobtrusively to undergo surgery in the nick of time. In his mind he had committed to do the lecture. And he would fulfil his commitment as long as he was able. Acute appendicitis would simply be an excuse not to do what is right.

The third characteristic that Chris expresses is his genuine interest in others and his wish to make a difference to their lives. This cannot be faked and is as real in Chris as are all his documented surfing and other achievements.

But in the end we come back to the single characteristic in Chris that I find so difficult to understand. It is this ability not to see the utter impossibility that I see in what he is trying to achieve. That is, until he achieves it and proves me wrong. Now I know better. If Chris believes it is possible, then it will happen regardless of my scepticism.

Consider his fastest crossing of the English Channel on a stand-up paddleboard. To do this, he went without sleep or food after finishing one challenge in the early hours of the morning – paddling the length of the Thames River – to begin the Channel crossing a few hours later, at first light. In those few hours he went without sleep or food, as he had left himself just enough time to travel from the finish of the one event to the start of the other.

Most people would say eat and sleep first, then paddle on another day. But that is not the nature of this man. When opportunity strikes, it must be taken. Like the time he surfed Mavericks with two broken ribs because he knew it was his only chance to show that he was good enough to be invited to that iconic competition. That he went on to win it is just a part of the Bertish legend.

I have been fortunate to meet some quite remarkable sportsmen and women in my life. A few stand out as being beyond extraordinary. Chris is one of them. This book describes his story. Read it and marvel. Then wonder how his message can impact on each one of our lives. And make us better as a result of his example and his unique wisdom.

PROFESSOR TIM NOAKES
CAPE TOWN, SOUTH AFRICA

Prologue

Mavericks, Northern California, February 2010

The wave looms above me, dark and cold and ominous. It's coming in fast and I realise my greatest fear is about to be realised.

I've just scratched my way over a deep-sea monster, reaching with everything I've got so I don't get sucked back over the 50-foot falls. The sound as the water detonates behind me is deafening.

As the spray starts to clear I look up, straining my eyes to see through the watery mist. My gut drops as I realise there is another wave coming. Unbelievably, unimaginably, this leviathan is even bigger than the last. And there's another one rising up after that.

How is this possible? I'm at least 150 metres further out than I've ever been in my 10 years of experience at this break. There is no way the next wave can be bigger than what I just paddled over. No way it can break even further out. But the more I strain my mind into believing it isn't going to happen, the more it insists that what I'm looking at is real. Right here, right now, within the next few crucial seconds, I'll be facing the exact situation I've been preparing for all my life – and been trying to avoid at all costs.

The waves here break so big and with such immense power that when they come crashing down, if you could harness the power of just one, it would light up a small town for a week. These

are the scariest waves I've ever seen. They are pure, raw, untamed open-ocean power. They are majestically beautiful – and will kill you if you get caught in the wrong place, or make a mistake or even a slight miscalculation.

Everything seems to shift into slow motion. There is nothing I can do to avoid the inevitable: there's a 65-foot wave bearing down on me, a moving four-storey building made of water (see the diagram on page 14), almost two kilometres wide and 20 metres tall. The lip of the wave is three metres wide, and it's about to thunder down directly onto my head.

Can this really be happening to me, in the first 10 minutes of my first heat of the coveted Mavericks Big Wave Invitational, after everything I've been through to get here?

It can take a lifetime to realise a dream and a matter of seconds to die trying to attain it. I look up at the thundering lip coming down and think, *If I actually survive this, if I live through what's about to happen, I can survive anything.* And that's when it hits me like a 10-ton truck … BOOM!

It had taken me more than 10 years – actually, my whole life – to get here. Everything I had been working towards came down to this exact moment. As the world went black, I thought, *Holy shit, I'm in really deep trouble. Could this be the end?*

But it was really only the beginning.

1

Beginnings

The old man and the sea

The ocean made me, just like it made my old man.

Keith Bertish was a real waterman. He was small in stature, but he was solid. Robust, stocky and hard as nails, with a big smile, a giant heart and courage to match. I remember him as fearless, always prepared, pure and true. A man who believed in the good of others, who believed in himself and in his power to do whatever he set his mind to. He taught his three boys to not follow the pack, to think out of the box and to blaze our own trails.

We grew up on the southern-most tip of Africa, in Cape Town, near the meeting point of two of the world's greatest oceans – the Indian and the Atlantic. We were blessed to have these two mighty oceans coming together right on our doorstep, bringing the waves and conditions to suit every kind of serious water lover.

The sea off Cape Town is raw, rough, rugged and wild. It can be harsh; get into the water here, whether you're a surfer or a sailor, and you should know you're climbing into an ocean that has claimed over 2 500 ships since the first one came here in the 15th century. This truly is the Cape of Storms.

Throw in gale-force winds, freezing cold water, strong currents, jagged reefs and more than a few great white sharks, and you have

1

pretty much the most treacherous marine environment you can imagine. It's an amazing place to grow up.

I only realised later in life, after travelling all over the world, that everywhere else feels pretty tame compared to Cape Town's coastline. Which is probably why I set out to find the biggest, scariest, most challenging waves on the planet, and to test myself in them.

I have my father to thank for that, too. He had an amazing feeling for the ocean, and he passed that on to me and my two older brothers, Greg and Conn. Keith waterskied for South Africa and Britain, he sailed all over the world, he won a leg of the Berg River Canoe Marathon, and he built the first ever catamaran in South Africa.

Some of my earliest memories are of sailing on that first home-made catamaran, named the *Tie Four*. From the age of five I would sail with my dad, often falling asleep high up on one hull, while the catamaran heeled over on the other. I was completely at peace, ocean sailing with my dad. It became like a second home, a place where I felt content, comfortable and free.

But as comfortable as I was in the ocean, I was taught to always approach it with the utmost respect and humility. That was how we three were raised: to be well mannered, respectful, courteous and humble. This was even more important given the wild time in which we grew up.

South Africa in the seventies was a bit like the Wild West, and luckily we had our father to lead us through it. He took us to some pretty hardcore places that most kids would never be exposed to. He took us to secret locations up the Skeleton Coast of Namibia to surf uncharted territory. We travelled to Botswana and through the Okavango Delta by *mokoro*, and trekked on foot through bush containing lion, hippo, crocodiles and rhino. I remember watching the eyes circling the campsite at night, praying that the fire wouldn't go out while I was on fire duty, everyone else huddled in their sleeping bags. I took the responsibility very seriously.

We were experiencing, sharing and learning all the time, about life, about the wild elements of nature, about the ocean, about ourselves, our limits, our borders and boundaries. We used to call it "Just go, Bertish!" time. It helped us forge a strong bond, especially between us brothers, a bond that my dad nurtured. He was so involved in our lives and he challenged us on every level. My father's first great lesson to us was to never accept anything less than the very best we could give. He believed life is for living, and told us to get out there and make things happen.

By walking a different road to most of our friends, we discovered things about ourselves, about who we were in this world, what we wanted to achieve and how we could contribute. We grew up knowing that we were privileged; we had a roof over our heads, which was a lot more than most. My father also taught us that it was common decency to give back every chance we got. If not for him, I know it would have been harder for me to do all the crazy things I'm going to tell you about in this book. He was a legend, a mentor, a father and a hero to his sons.

Of course none of this would have been possible without my mom. She was like a rock, solid in the background, keeping it all together, keeping the home fires burning. I owe a great debt not only to my mother and father, but also to the two incredibly astute, amazingly supportive and special people I'm proud to call my brothers.

Blood brothers

We were always in the water, sailing, skiing, surfing, windsurfing, fishing – we did it all, together. Because my dad was always on the ocean, we learnt to do most things three or four years before other kids. And because I was the youngest, when my brothers learnt, I wanted to learn at the same time. I became a determined little guy, trying to keep up and be as good as my brothers. *Not* keeping up was never an option!

The three of us were a pretty formidable little team. There is a two-year difference between each of us. As the youngest, I wanted to be as good as them in everything they did; better, if possible. I guess this made me super driven, super determined and super focused – I had to be, otherwise I got left behind!

I challenged myself to keep up with them from the moment I could walk. Greg would start something, Conn would take it a bit further and then I would just try to keep up with both of them.

By the age of five I was already an accomplished waterskier. There were no skis small enough for me at the time, so my father made a pair out of wood. I still have them today; they are the smallest, funniest little things you have ever seen.

By seven I was windsurfing, even though I battled to lift up the kiddies' rig. By the time I was nine, I was surfing.

That drive to keep up with my brothers and be in the ocean as much as possible taught me at an early age that if I set my mind to something and was truly focused on it, I could achieve almost anything. Once I realised that, I just wanted to be good at every-thing, whether it was school athletics, rugby, sailing, windsurfing or surfing.

I started to develop a strong work ethic, which also helped me during the times I battled at school. My brothers still tease me about the fact that when I get an idea in my head I become so focused, it's as if I have tunnel vision.

A lot of my childhood memories were forged in Langebaan lagoon, 120 kilometres up the West Coast from Cape Town. My family had a little bungalow, one of the first houses there; this tiny shack by the water was the base from which my father taught us to respect the ocean, the weather, our environment and everything in it.

My earliest childhood memories are of the ocean. I loved learning from it and trying to figure out its various moods, how it moved and breathed. I learnt to flow with it, not fight against it, to let it help me rather than hinder me. I loved all its moods and how it was constantly changing. I learnt that in life I needed to be flexible and change like the ocean, to feel and experience the freedom that it offered.

My brothers and I had a gang called the Wild Cats, and we used to get up to all sorts of trouble. For a couple of years we scared the hell out of the tourists at Langebaan by towing a fake shark fin behind our little rowboat in the lagoon. The first fin we made was a bit small, but it was classic; it was weighted wrongly, so when we paddled fast it would flop over and look like the shark had gone under for the kill.

But the second one Greg shaped was a real masterpiece; it was scary, realistic and beautiful, and we caused mayhem with this big, bad boy. At one point we even had the navy come out and try to take pot shots at it – they thought a shark was about to attack three little boys in a dinghy, never realising that we were actually towing the fin behind us with fishing line.

When I was 10 years old, the big guy in the red suit (my dad loved to play this role) left us each a four-foot polystyrene surfboard under the Christmas tree. I don't know if they were actually meant to be surfed, but in our house, if it floated, the Bertish boys would try to stand on it. We surfed those little boards until they fell apart, or in my case until I tried to windsurf on it and the mast fell right through and broke it in half. I was already learning that you never know unless you try ...

It wasn't long before we upgraded to real surfboards. There was nothing like packing up the VW Kombi with my dad and my brothers and heading up the West Coast to Elands Bay. Back then it was still pretty rustic – no tar roads, all gravel, just a handful of houses, the campsite and the old faithful Elands Bay Hotel. Surf, camp, catch crayfish, tell campfire stories, eat, sleep, repeat!

As we moved into our early teens we started doing trips further up the coast, as far as the "diamond area" and Cape Cross in Namibia. All in search of the perfect wave.

Every so often my brothers and I still disappear up the coast together for a few days to reconnect. Our bond is important to us. It's the unique bond of three; like the corners of a triangle that give one another strength and in turn give the triangle its strength. Our passion for the ocean and for riding waves together keeps us grounded and connected, as friends and as brothers, at the core.

Surfing

I started surfing competitively when I was about 12. Not everyone was so thrilled with my passion for waves; many of my teachers at school had the wrong image of surfing. They saw it as a distraction, and wanted me to dedicate myself to more traditional mainstream sports like rugby. They had no idea how serious I was about surfing!

In my world, it's a real problem if I'm not able to get my training done or get in the water every couple of days. I lose my balance, my grounding, my sanity. In somebody else's world, it's serious if they aren't meeting targets at work. It's all relative. Serious means different things to different people. An early lesson for me was how society wants you to fit into this little box, and dictate to you how you should behave to be "normal" and fit in.

That was when I first realised that it's so important to follow your own passions, dreams and beliefs. To do what's important to you, and not what other people think is important for you. I don't believe in sending people down the path that everyone else has taken. Why on earth would you want to be like everyone else? We should all strive to be unique and evolve our own talents. Just focus on being the best exceptional you that you can be, and leave a legacy.

I'm very glad I didn't listen to anybody else when it came to my own life.

Society has this idea that surfing is not a serious pursuit. They think it's a dropout sport for teens in little rubber suits who smoke too much. They still seem to associate it with rebels who are constantly bunking school. That's just an old cliché. Like all clichés, it might be based on a grain of truth. But it's not the whole truth – in fact, it has always proved the complete opposite for me. Surfing has kept me honest, grounded, fit and lean, it's taught me wisdom, taken me on great adventures and kept me true.

Surfing was not just something I was good at. It was something I was incredibly passionate about. I felt I was born to be a fish, to be in the ocean in any shape or form – I often joke that I was supposed to be amphibious, except that God forgot to give me gills!

The ocean was a place where I was free to express myself, to test myself with no limits – not like on land, where there are so many rules and restrictions, so many people trying to tell you what you can and cannot achieve. In the ocean you are truly free; alone yet connected to yourself and nature in its purest form. It's a clean canvas on which you can discover yourself, create your own magic and push your limits as far as you can. It's the ultimate testing ground.

Too often we let our childhood dreams slip away because we are told to grow up, settle down, get serious and get real about life. The really serious ones, in my opinion, are the ones who never give up on their dreams, the ones who never give in and never let go but keep pursuing and chasing them, always.

Nobody can tell me that big-wave surfing is not a serious pursuit. I think there's something pretty serious about surfing waves so big, they can kill you in a heartbeat. And it wasn't long before I realised that those really big waves were the ones I wanted to test myself against.

2

The bigger the better

Outer Kom

I'll never forget the first time I surfed the Outer Kom. I was 13 years old and out with my brothers. The waves seemed massive, even though they were probably only around two metres or so. But for the first time in my life the ocean felt really daunting, scary and threatening.

We all got caught inside a few times, but then I got separated from my brothers and, by the time I popped up to the surface, after the third wave hit me, I was in tears and filled with panic. That's when I made my first big mistake in big-wave surfing: I decided to try to catch the white water back to shore. When you're surfing bigger waves, it's never a good idea to turn around and try to catch the white water lying down, no matter how easy it might seem at the time, because you are going to get hammered. Sometimes the only thing you can do when you get caught inside by a big wave is to ditch your board, swim down as deep as you can, open your eyes and try to get under the turbulence. Hard as it may seem, you need to relax and go with the flow, not fight it. The ocean is bigger than you are; you need to work with its energy.

It takes experience to know that the seemingly easy way out of a tough situation can often get you into even more trouble.

I didn't have that experience yet, but I soon figured out that sometimes you have to push even deeper through an obstacle to get out safely on the other side.

My first experience of big waves at the Outer Kom was the first time I was completely out of my comfort zone in the ocean, and even though it scared me and freaked me out, somehow I got hooked. I was drawn to it, challenged by it. It was like a beast that I wanted to tame. I wanted more.

Slowly, I started to put myself into bigger and bigger surf. Slowly, I became more comfortable. As I got the hang of it, I began to get more confident.

The first time we do something we'll always be out of our comfort zone, and that may seem scary. But I believe that the best way to become good at anything is to take that leap of faith and face your fears head-on. With time you start to realise that they're not that scary any more. When they become familiar, they become your new comfort zone. That's when you can take it up a notch and start pushing yourself even further.

I call it "shifting my comfort zone", and it's how I was able to go on and surf some of the world's biggest and scariest waves. Some people may think I'm crazy doing what I do, but the definition of crazy is different for everybody. I personally think cycling in traffic is completely nuts. Climbing onto a bike on our roads, riding with your back to what's coming up behind you, putting your faith in those drivers when you are blind to what's coming and aren't able to take evasive action – now *that's* completely crazy! At least I can see my big wave coming.

"Crazy" is what people call something or someone they don't understand, something that doesn't fit their sense of what is "normal". Something that is out of their personal comfort zone and challenges their frame of reference.

Surfing 20- to 30-foot face waves is completely normal for me now. It's my happy place, where I feel calm, content, relaxed and free. Over time, it's come to fit right into my comfort zone and I don't think anything of it. But 50- to 60-foot face waves are another story – they still challenge me and every other surfer on this planet who dares to face them! The thing is, it's rare to get precisely the right day and conditions for these waves, so it's really difficult to get accustomed to riding them on a regular basis – otherwise our comfort zone probably would have shifted around them, too.

So everybody's level of crazy, the boundaries of their comfort zone, and what they perceive to be risky and difficult really just depend on their relative frame of reference, how much time, effort and experience they have in a particular situation to eventually make it their norm. I've put time, research and huge amounts of planning, training and preparation into big-wave surfing. I've built up decades of experience, refined my equipment and minimised the risks so that I can proceed with confidence.

Riding those petrifying first waves at Outer Kom, I had no idea that big waves would become my life's main mission. But my passion for surfing just grew and grew. My brothers were a massive inspiration. Our friends used to joke that you don't try to go bigger than the Bertish brothers because otherwise you'll get hurt.

And then there were surfers like Pierre de Villiers, Jonathan Paarman, Ian Armstrong, Cass Collier and Mickey Duffus. These were the pioneers of Cape Town's big-wave hotspots: Dungeons, Sunset, Outer Kom and the Crayfish Factory. Watching and learning from these guys, and surfing with my brothers, played a major role in my development.

There is a saying that great people stand on the shoulders of giants. The greats of the past help us reach greatness ourselves. If you have the opportunity, learn from them as much as you possibly can. Wisdom comes from knowledge, knowledge comes from

experience and experience comes from making mistakes or learning from others that have made them. Watch and learn. Then make fewer mistakes.

I've learnt more from the school of life and the ocean than any formal educational institution could ever have taught me. And my greatest teachers were ordinary men who spent each day challenging themselves, learning from the ocean and going beyond their limits. I was young and really looked up to these guys. I wanted to be just like them, perhaps better.

If you start to see life as your school and an opportunity to learn on a daily basis, then you quickly realise that there is no such thing as failure, only a failure to try. A mistake is only a mistake if you make it twice. When it came to surfing the big waves, I soon realised that the stakes are so high you often won't get the luxury of being able to make the same mistake twice, so you better take it seriously and learn the first time!

But maybe to better understand this principle, I need to tell you a little about the waves themselves.

Wave science

The waves I travel the world to surf begin far out, deep within the ocean. They are born from the wild winds where huge storms unleash their energy, penetrating down into the depths. I imagine them as dragons that come roaring in from the deep, frothing and spitting as the seafloor rises up to meet them. That's when they ascend with the almighty power and majesty of Poseidon himself, towering over those of us mortals who have paddled out to meet them.

Each cubic metre of water weighs a little over one ton. So you quite often find yourself staring up at a wall of water weighing in at over 500 tons. Imagine how it would feel if 300 cars were dropped on your head. The bigger the wave, the faster it moves, so these big boys are moving at speeds of between 30 and 50 kilometres per hour.

When you're riding down and across these giant beasts, you're going twice as fast as this. Get it right, and you're in for the adrenaline rush and thrill of your lifetime. Get it wrong, and the force of one of these waves can push you down over 12 metres deep in a split second, and hold you there for over a minute with a force that feels like it's trying to rip you limb from limb.

All this time you're remembering not to panic, even though you're underwater and will only be able to get to the surface to breathe when the ocean allows you to, and not when you choose. This is one environment in which you are never 100 per cent in control and the ocean will always rule supreme.

If you don't make it to the surface in time, lack of oxygen will eventually cause you to black out. Once you black out, your brain can go without oxygen for anywhere between two and four minutes before you are clinically dead. And even if you do survive a blackout, there is a real chance of sustaining brain damage. When you're facing a reality like this, being all you can be and chasing your dreams can seem like a really stupid idea. Maybe that's why at any one time there are fewer than 50 or so hardened big-wave warriors around the world who chase this passion as their livelihood.

You can fit that number of people into a single Table Mountain cable car. This small group of serious watermen is the true core of big-wave surfing on the planet.

We actively chase these waves, year round, keeping one eye on the weather chart, looking out for the colours that will signal the perfect storm, training non-stop to be prepared to drop everything at any moment and go where we must to meet the waves we crave. Waves with names like Jaws, Ghost Trees, Dungeons, Mavericks, the Cribbar and Killers.

How did I become one of these?

It helped that I grew up in the ideal surfing playground. Cape Town is unique in terms of its surfing options. There's a surf spot for every size of wave and every kind of condition. And it has the perfect starter waves as stepping stones to get into bigger surf.

WAVE HEIGHT and SCALE

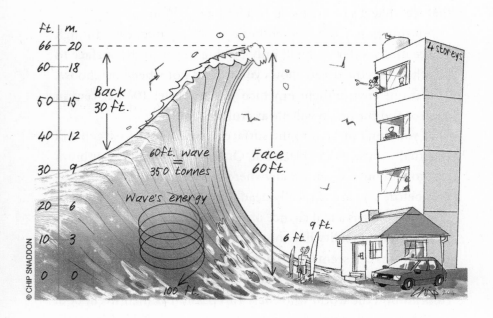

All the big-wave spots in South Africa – namely Outer Kom, the Crayfish Factory, Sunset and Dungeons – are within a 10-kilometre radius, which is incredibly unique. Most of the world's big-wave spots stand alone and stick out like sore thumbs from everything else around them – or certainly any other big waves of consequence. But here we have these four amazing big-wave surf spots, all relatively close to one another, all working in different wind and swell conditions, and each leading to the next in terms of difficulty.

Of course, I didn't see the specialness back then, but I recognise it now.

The Kom is your medium-entry-level big-wave spot. It breaks from 6 to 12 feet, mostly with a southerly and south-westerly swell and south-southeast wind direction. It's relatively safe and has a big channel; you get flushed into the rocks and then Inner Kom, which is a baby wave where people learn to surf on the inside. It's fairly sheltered and fairly consistent in the bigger swells of the winter.

Your next wave, the Crayfish Factory, is just three kilometres around the corner and works on a completely different wind direction – north-northwest – and different swell conditions. So, whereas the Kom works in summer and winter, and only needs a medium-size swell and a light southeaster, the Factory only works in the heart of winter, when you have the strong north-westerly winter storms coming in, creating bigger swells. The sea gets wild and rugged, but the Factory produces these beautiful groomed lines of surf.

It's a tricky, technical wave to surf; there are shallow sections, which create steps in the wave that make it quite challenging. The Factory might not be as powerful and scary as some of the other big-wave spots, but the steps add an interesting element that you need to get your head around.

The wave peels off an actual (now non-operational) crayfish factory that sticks out into the sea, so when you're out there you feel like you're in the middle of the ocean. You are surrounded by a big open bay on one side; if your leash snaps you'll get washed into a channel that flushes out into the middle of this bay, so you need to be mindful and learn about the currents here. At 8 to 15 feet, it's a proper wave of consequence; a lot of people don't realise how dangerous it is. When the waves here get to that size, you're not able to swim against the current.

Most surf spots have a rip so that if you get into trouble, you can find your way out fairly easily. Not the Factory; get into trouble here and you will very quickly learn just how powerful the ocean is.

And then you get Sunset, which also works in the light summer southeaster, but needs the bigger winter swells. Sunset is a perfect A-frame peak that breaks almost two kilometres out at sea, which means it's remote and very exposed to the wind. The peak is so refined it breaks in the same place most of the time – it just gets further out the bigger it breaks, so it goes from being an 8- to 10-foot wave to as big as the ocean can deliver. It's one of those amazing, majestic waves; so pretty and perfect when conditions are right, but evil, ominous, powerful and scary when they're not.

When things go wrong here you realise just how exposed you are, because the playing field gets exponentially larger; when you fall here and the other surfers are out at the back, they are literally almost a kilometre away from you so they have no idea that you are in trouble. In a way, Sunset reminds me of a prettier version of Mavericks – it's still a heavy big-wave spot, but it doesn't have as intense an impact zone. Mavericks is incredibly focused and draws all its energy into one point. Sunset does that, too, but not to the same magnitude. So if you ever want to prepare for Mavericks, Sunset is a slightly tamer version – although when you're out there looking at it breaking at 20 feet, you would never think of calling it tame!

Last but not least we have Dungeons, our winter big wave. Dungeons breaks off a mountain called the Sentinel, which anchors one side of Hout Bay harbour. You have to take a boat out or walk over a mountain to get to it. It breaks one and a half kilometres offshore, near a seal colony. It has lots of wild and raw elements (including sharks), and a massive open-ocean channel on the side.

It's such a unique wave and has so many take-off points that

I don't consider it a typical big-wave spot. A normal big wave has a zone where you sit out and wait; Dungeons has three or four take-off spots within that zone, making the playing field exponentially wider and more open. It's difficult to work out how to be in the right place to catch the wave, to know how the ocean moves and breathes here. Every single time you surf Dungeons, it's different. This makes Dungeons incredibly challenging. It's not a question of *if* you are going to get caught inside, but rather how many times. If you get caught inside at any of the other big-wave spots, it's because you haven't read it right, or because you got hit by an unusually large set. With Dungeons you're never sure whether you're in the right place. And even if you are in the right place, you can take off on a wave, ride it to the point where you think you have finished your ride, then pull out of it and still get hit by another 20-foot wave.

These are the four that make up the Cape Town surfer's big-wave school. You use the Kom as a foundation, then move on to the Factory. You get a feel for the technical, powerful ledgey barrels, how the ocean moves and breathes; you get into trouble and you learn how to get out of it. From there you move on to Sunset, where the waves are generally bigger, but also more precise and readable, which makes them more manageable. And finally you get to Dungeons, where everything you learnt from the last three sort of goes out the window and you think, *Whoa, what's this?* It's a whole different kind of animal.

Dungeons is a big part of the reason why South Africans who go over to the big-wave spots in Hawaii or California do really well; our environment here is so raw, the conditions are so bumpy, windy, wild and hectic. It's as if the wildness of the African land-scape is absorbed into our seas.

Predicting the unpredictable

Big-wave surfing is a passion, an obsession, a love and an addiction that's hard to explain. Riding the dragons of the deep is what drives us; it's how we're hardwired and what we are born to do.

People would sometimes tell me that I was going too far, that I was too focused on it, that I should give myself a break. But if you want to be the best, then only you know exactly how far you have to go, and what you need to do and are willing to sacrifice to get there. With dedication to your dreams also comes great sacrifice.

The extreme environment of big-wave surfing is something completely unique. There is no other major sport where the environment is so volatile, deadly, scary and constantly changing. It's not like a tennis court or a football field where you have set parameters and you're playing within a set, constant space. Those playing fields don't change overnight; they don't move or double in size; they don't have wild animals released onto them, suddenly, without warning.

The big-wave surfing arena is massive and always in flux. It's moved by the current; it changes according to wind, tide, swell size, period and direction, where the waves are breaking and how far they have travelled. This variability, and its inherent challenges, makes big-wave surfing a fascinating art, as well as a science. You have to be totally in tune, focused and 100 per cent in the moment in order to survive.

You can go out to the same location day after day and the conditions will be completely different each time. Every storm alters the intensity of the waves and how and where they break. Every wave you paddle into is unique; there is no single wave alike, and you therefore have to adjust your skill, strategy and reactions to read that wave every time you get to your feet.

A tennis player can plan to practise every single day. A runner can fit a quick jog into a lunch break. But it's not possible to go out and train in big-wave surf every day, because there aren't big waves every day. That doesn't mean you never train; it means you have to train all the time.

And you don't just train for the good days but, more importantly, for the serious days, the really big days when things can go horribly wrong. You train for those rare days when conditions look like they are going to be right, but change suddenly and dramatically to become so dangerous that it takes all you've got to get out of there alive. If you have a bad day as a rugby player or tennis player or golfer, you mark it down as a bad day, wipe it aside, learn from it and try again tomorrow. But a bad day in big-wave surfing can mean you don't play again, ever!

Being at your best, at your physical peak, every time it counts, all the time, makes big-wave surfing a phenomenally challenging sport. On a good day, you come back with "Stoked!" written all over your face. But if you're not prepared, a bad day in this sport is one in which you don't come home at all.

As big-wave surfers, we have no fixed competition date. We are on standby all the time, 24/7, 365 days of the year, ready to drop anything and everything with 24 to 48 hours' notice of a major event, get on a flight within hours and fly halfway around the world when the conditions are suddenly right. When that happens the window to ride these waves is often only four to six hours; that's when the conditions are not too dangerous or life-threatening, not too windy, not too stormy; when the tide, the wind, the swell – everything – is just right.

This means you have to be super focused, committed, vigilant, disciplined and consistent in your preparation and training. At the same time you need to be incredibly flexible, constantly adjusting to new situations, changing plans and making sacrifices all the time. Everything, your entire world, revolves around what's happening out in the ocean and with the weather that stirs it up.

There are days when I would love to just go out and surf the whole morning, just enjoy myself in the ocean rather than go to the gym and put in the effort doing my underwater and cardio-vascular training. It's tough sometimes, making those choices, when the easier option is a lot more fun. It's tough to always be the one having a non-alcoholic beer at a braai with your friends for months on end, because there's big surf on its way in the morning or because you're on standby for an event. It's tough getting up early every morning, leaving jobs because you need more flexible hours, getting into debt, breaking up with girlfriends because they don't understand what drives you ...

But when you know where you are headed, it becomes a whole lot easier to make the sacrifices that will lead to your success (and possibly save your life). Once you find your "why", everything else falls into place.

The first stoke is the deepest

When I was 17, there was a key moment when the ocean truly humbled me. We were surfing the Crayfish Factory, probably one of my favourite big-wave spots still to this day. It was a pretty big day for me at that point in my life and the waves were in the 20- to 25-foot face range. It was definitely pushing my comfort zone, but it was super clean. I was scared, but I was still itching with anticipation to get out there, as I knew it was set to be a truly epic day.

I was surfing with my brother and some of my mentors, Ian, Mickey and Cass. A big set came in, sparkling in the sunlight, and it was beautiful. The set stood up and one of the legends got the first one, but the second one was all mine ... I was a little appre-hensive, but I was in the perfect spot and I knew I wanted it. I was determined to catch it and ride it. I was going, no matter what.

I took off late, sliding down the massive wall, just managing to hold my edge as it started to lurch, stand up and come thundering down behind me. As I came down and drew a long arc off the bottom, I could see up ahead that it was forming a massive cavernous barrel. I knew that if I dropped the rail of my board and straightened out, the lip would land square on me, so my next best and safest option was to pull up into this grinding, moving cauldron. I set my rail and pulled up high, into the huge gaping, spinning and tunnelling (tube) wave. I remember being inside it and thinking, *This is unbelievable, this is insane, this is the most amazing sight, sound and feeling I've ever experienced!*

I felt like I was in a big, green, spinning ocean cathedral, and it was huge and beautiful, like a whirling glimpse of heaven. The image and experience was so powerful, as everything else slowed down, that it became crystal clear and imprinted in my brain forever. I tried to see if I could ride through and out of that barrel, but I knew I was too deep. I remember thinking, *I want more of this feeling, this is incredible.* And then I got hammered.

I got pushed down deep pretty quick and my surfboard's leash got tangled around a piece of kelp. I started to panic as I reached down to try to untangle it. I could see the surface three feet above me, but I felt my oxygen running out just when my leash finally came loose. When I surfaced I was pretty freaked out, but simultaneously incredibly stoked! I couldn't contain my joy. Every one of my senses was buzzing and on hyper-drive. It was an adrenaline rush like nothing I had experienced before, and I had a massive grin on my face for ages afterwards. I knew right then that I wanted more of that feeling. I wanted to pull into big, badass, gaping barrels of terror as often as I could!

As luck would have it, there was a photographer out there that day. He captured a sequence of images of me pulling up into the barrel with my hands above my head. It went into a couple of

magazines and made an instant impression on the South African surfing scene – not many people pulled into big, gaping closeout barrels in those days. They still don't. Conn told me later that he and Greg were on the beach and saw me catch that wave. They looked at each other as if to say, "Wow, Chris has turned a corner here; that's a whole other level."

They were right. It was a major turning point for me. That day made me realise I could be as good as, if not better than, some of the best big-wave surfers. At the very least I was going to give it a try. I was going to push myself and my comfort zone as often as I could, and see where it would take me.

I didn't know it at the time, but that feeling, that incredible split-second feeling riding inside that beast, had hooked me and changed my life forever.

Days that haunt you

There are moments in life that stay with you forever; times when reality kicks in and demands the very best from you. How you react in those situations, no matter what the outcome – good or bad – can haunt you forever.

One of these key moments in my life was during another session surfing the Factory, about two years later. There were just a few of us out, including a friend of mine, Andrew Preen. Andrew was a really good surfer and someone I looked up to and respected immensely. He was about four years older than me and surfed big waves really well. He was one of those solid, all-round surfers who could hold their own in anything, something I had always aspired to be.

That day we were surfing 15- to 20-foot face waves, with some sets coming through even bigger than that. After about 45 minutes a solid set came in and caught Andrew and me inside. It was pretty average by my standards today, nothing to be really stressed about, but still a big wave that demanded respect.

Andrew and I were a few metres apart in the water and we both knew we were going to be caught. I even laughed just before we were about to get hammered, and said, "Shit, we're in trouble now!" We bailed our boards to the side and swam down to try to get under it. I remember being under for quite a while, but somehow coming up a little quicker than I had expected. I managed to get another two breaths in before the next big wave in the set landed on my head.

I got to my board after that one, and managed to quickly scratch up and over the next wave just before it caught me. I paddled over the top as it was breaking and looked back to see if Andrew had managed to get through. That's when I saw his board tomb-stoning; its nose still half underwater and sticking straight up, meaning he was still deep beneath the water and hadn't surfaced yet. This was a really bad sign. It meant he'd already had a two-wave hold-down and if he didn't surface before the one I was paddling over, that would be three. I knew right then and there that if he didn't surface before the third one, the likelihood of him surviving was very slim. A two-wave hold-down is rare, but no one I know of has ever survived three.

As big-wave surfers, we're like a brotherhood. We really look out for one another out there. The ocean is a powerful and humbling place and things can go from good to very bad in a split second. When they do, you'd better be ready, prepared and able to deal with it, as the situation could irrevocably change your life, or someone else's, forever.

After paddling over that wave, I turned my board round to face Andrew's position, looking towards the impact zone and then the beach, watching to see if he was going to surface. I looked back

towards the ocean and saw the next couple of waves coming, but I didn't care. I could take it – I just wanted to get to Andrew. He still hadn't surfaced, which meant I was already dealing with an unconscious situation, and if I couldn't get to him quickly, it would change into the worst-case scenario: he would be dead and his body would be taking in water. No matter what I did, it was going to take me time, too much time, to get him to shore, where I would be able to revive him. I had already begun to realise that even if I could get to him quickly, so far from shore the odds were slim at best, even if things went well.

Paddling back into the impact zone was frightening, but it was the least of my worries at that moment. I reached Andrew's board after another two waves had hit me and he was still underwater – shit, it must have been at least three minutes by now. I pulled him up by his leash and got him to the surface just as the next big wall of white water hit us.

I tried with all my might to hold onto him, but holding up a lifeless 90-kilogram body when you are being battered around underwater by 12 feet of turbulent ocean, which is trying to take your life as well, was beyond anything I had ever imagined. But even harder was feeling the ocean ripping him from my grasp, knowing that, as hard as I was trying to hold him, I just didn't have the power or the energy to resist the ocean. Even today, 15 years later, I have flashbacks to that horrendous feeling of my hands slipping as the ocean tore my friend's lifeless body away from me. After fighting so hard to get to him and get him up, I just couldn't hold onto him.

I came up gasping for air and immediately looked around for Andrew. Once I saw him it still took another two waves to get back to him. I tried holding him again through the white water, but it was futile. The ocean was too strong and I was getting weaker trying to keep him at the surface. By now there was foam coming from his mouth and his face and lips had turned purple and blue. As I was shouting at him to stay with me, I was thinking that if I didn't get us out of this situation pretty quickly, there was no way he would survive.

I realised the only way I could try to stick with him was to tangle my leash around his board and leash. Once I had done this, I knew we couldn't be separated, even if I couldn't hold him. But that led to the next problem: as the next wave hit, it smashed one of the tangled boards into my head, almost knocking me unconscious. By then I realised I just *had* to hold on, because I was almost through the worst of it, even though the onslaught seemed relentless. If I could get us through another couple of waves, with Andrew still attached to me, we would be out of the main impact zone and I could get him to the channel, get some rescue breaths in, try to pump his stomach, call for help, and get him to the beach as soon as possible to try to revive him on land.

After another two waves, the set had moved through and past us, and subsided enough for me to drag him onto my board and paddle him into the channel. I called for help while trying to clear his airway and gave him two rescue breaths. One of my brothers helped me to get Andrew to land. But by the time we reached the beach, I was pretty sure he was dead. I remember giving him CPR, and I did get him to come around after another four to five minutes, but his eyes had this horrible milkiness to them.

I was sure that even if we got him back, he'd been dead for so long now – over 10 minutes, I reckoned – that he would definitely have brain damage. Still, I managed to get him stable, warm and out of the wind, and kept reassuring him until the emergency services arrived about 20 minutes later. The ambulance took him straight to Mediclinic Constantiaberg, where he spent the next couple of days in intensive care.

I went in to see Andrew in ICU that afternoon, but he was

sleeping, his body exhausted and traumatised. My mind was pretty traumatised from the whole experience, too. It had been horrific and terrifying; I wouldn't wish that experience on my worst enemy.

Andrew made it, miraculously. It shouldn't be possible for him to still be alive today without brain damage, but I guess there was something bigger than us at play that day. And I know it could just as easily have been me instead of Preeny.

In some ways, I think it was worse for me, because to this day he doesn't remember much past the second wave passing over him. But I remember every moment, every millisecond that seemed to last a lifetime; it still haunts me to this day.

When he came out of hospital, Andrew didn't surf big waves for four or five years, but I'm stoked to say he's surfing them again now. As for me, I learnt a couple of really valuable lessons that day, one of which was that no matter how desperate things seem at the time in a hectic situation, never, ever give up, as there's always hope. It also brought to the forefront how the ocean is to be respected, no matter the size of the waves.

But even though the experience haunted me, I was still hungry to surf bigger waves. I still wanted more.

Hard loss

I'm a great believer that you should prepare for the worst and hope for the best. Preparing for the worst is not pessimistic or negative thinking – unless you are acting out of fear. My experience with Andrew at the Factory just confirmed for me how important it is to be ready to deal with any emergency at any time. Inevitably, something will go wrong in life. When it does, you can take confidence from the fact that you are fit, ready and mentally prepared for it, and can make quick, clear and rational decisions. It won't stop the hurt or the heartache. But it will help you get through it, and it could change the outcome to a positive one. It could possibly save someone else's life.

Having said that, there are some situations for which you can never be prepared.

I was 21 when my father passed away. It was tough on all of us. My father was such a larger-than-life presence. He did everything with us and shared so much of himself with us, in every way. It was even more traumatic for me because I was there the day it happened.

He had been working too hard. He knew it and had set a date for when he was going to slow down and relax more, take time off and hand over more of his business to his staff and partner. Friday marked the end of his week and his date for this change. He said he knew it was time to relax and let go, and I think his mind and body decided to do just that.

I was studying inside the house for my exams when I heard a loud thud outside. My father had been cutting some low branches from a tree next to the house when he collapsed. He had suffered a major heart attack. I had emergency services training and began to do my absolute best to resuscitate him. I'd already resuscitated a few surfers and other people in the past. But as hard as I tried, whatever I did, no matter how much I wanted it to work this time round, more than ever before, I just couldn't bring him back.

Often in life the greatest growth lies in our weakest or lowest moments. That feeling of knowing I had saved so many other people before, but not being able to do so for my own father, my hero, my idol, was a devastating blow. Even though I didn't show it that day, as I had to remain strong for my mom, my brothers, my family, it was the only time in my life I have ever felt completely powerless and helpless. Nothing that I did, no matter how hard I

tried, no matter my training and all my experience, nothing would change the outcome.

You go over so many things in your head, time and time again, for days, months, years following that moment, trying to figure out how and where you might have gone wrong or made a mistake, how you could have done it better, got there quicker. Was the method I used 100 per cent right and what might I have done differently? This can be a dangerous exercise, because by trying to make sense of it all, you can end up blaming yourself for something over which you never had any control.

I've since come to accept that I did everything I possibly could that day, that sometimes in life there are things that are beyond our control and that we have to be able to let them go. What will be, will be.

When you lose in life, don't lose the lesson; in this case the lesson was that some things in life are simply beyond my control.

My captain, my father, my hero, my friend. I will always miss him. He was small in stature, but great in strength, heart and courage. He believed in the good of others. He believed in himself and the power of the mind. He always chose the path less travelled; never the one that was easy, but the one that was right. His determination, honesty, loyalty to his word and strength of character never failed him. I couldn't have picked a greater dad.

How fortunate I am that his spirit, his inspiring and adventurous ways, his special qualities rubbed off on each of his three sons. There isn't a day that goes by when I don't think fondly of him. I know he would have been proud of his boys. Losing him was the hardest thing in my life. Not being able to save him, when he had saved me so many times, was the most painful thing of all. But I know that he would tell me that I gave it my all, and that sometimes, when even your best isn't good enough, you just have to accept that there were greater powers at work.

3

Seeding the dream

Travels

After I finished school, I spent the next few years travelling. I sailed all over the world to pay my way, and surfed whenever and wherever I got the chance. It's only looking back that I can see I was planting the seeds of my dream.

I visited America, Brazil, the Caribbean and Europe, and sailed across the Atlantic and back delivering yachts. I learnt a great deal from those transatlantic trips, about myself, about what's important in life, about the magnitude and vastness of the ocean and how quickly things can change when you're out there. One day it's perfectly calm, glassy and peaceful, the next you have huge 40-foot swells and 50-knot winds and you are hanging on for dear life, feeling like a pawn in the middle of the ocean, insignificant and very much alone.

The ocean has a way of humbling you and keeping you grounded, connecting you and making you appreciative of everything you have. On those crossings, I really found myself, my happy place and my centre of complete calm, contentment and freedom. The ocean connects you to nature and the elements all around you. Realising your place in it all, and your absolute insignificance, gives you an amazing sense of peace.

After a lot of travelling by sea, I ended up working on a kibbutz in Israel, where I found myself constantly saving swimmers who had got themselves into trouble at their local beach. After this I headed down to the Red Sea, where I worked on a charter boat, and then to a place I had always dreamt of going: the great pyramids of Egypt. After crossing into Egypt, the tour guide stopped the bus at a rest stop, where we were offered a puff on a big hubbly-bubbly pipe that stood one and a half metres tall. I wasn't aware that it had hashish inside. I thought I would give it a try and put it down to new experiences, so I sucked on that pipe a couple of times and watched the stuff burn into coals as it went up in smoke, the eyes of the guide getting bigger and bigger. Apparently I was only meant to have a small, quick puff, as the stuff is so ridiculously strong.

Well, I certainly felt it! Within five minutes I wasn't able to stand up. I was shaking all over, and the bus almost left me behind while I was in the bathroom throwing up and turning a Kermit the Frog shade of green. I spent the remainder of the six-hour ride lying on the floor of the bus, shaking and trembling and totally stoned on stuff that I will never, ever touch again. You never know unless you try, but … everything in moderation!

I was running out of money, so I headed up to Murcia in south-west Spain. My aunt ran a small sailing school in a seaside town called La Manga, and I had just enough money to buy a train ticket down there. But the train only went halfway – which I found out when it stopped and everyone got out. I was told that a special train, which only came once every three days, would continue on from there at an additional cost. This special train would arrive and leave in two hours' time – and then not run again for a couple of days.

I was stuck about six hours away from where I needed to be with absolutely no money for the rest of the train trip. Broke, and no credit cards to rely on. Just an attitude and a mentality that said

I needed to suck it up, calm down, not panic, think rationally and make a plan, quickly. How could I get enough money together fast, like really fast, in a country where I couldn't speak the language and didn't know anyone? I had just an hour and 59 minutes and counting before I missed the only connecting train in three days.

Okay, calm down, Bertish. Think clearly: how to solve this, quickly. It's like a puzzle, it's a challenge – figure it out!

Growing up in South Africa taught me to be resourceful, so I opened up my backpack, grabbed my little Spanish/English dictionary, looked up some key words, got a piece of cardboard and wrote on it: "*Vende, desperado!*" (To sell, desperate!) I took out my running shoes and some T-shirts and CDs and began selling everything I could.

I still didn't have enough money for the ticket when the train pulled into the station, but I literally got down on my knees and pleaded with the lady behind the counter to sell me a ticket for what I had. She took pity on me, smiled and paid the difference herself. "*Vaya con Dios,*" she told me as she handed me the ticket. It was a gentle reminder that there are always angels out there, people who will help if they see you are in a difficult place but are still making the effort to try. If you ask for help and you genuinely need it, people will help you more often than you think. There is still plenty of good out there. (I would meet another angel behind a ticket counter at a big turning point in my life, but that was still some years away ...)

I boarded the train just in time and travelled to my aunt's place, where I spent six months teaching sailing and met an amazing Spanish girl who inspired me to learn the language a whole lot quicker. For a while I thought I might settle down with a beautiful Spanish woman and eat paella, teach sailing and grow old, lazy and fat drinking beer, and watching the boats sail by and the sun going down. But life had other plans for me.

Time goes by and things may change, but your deepest dreams and goals stay constant. As much as I look back fondly on those times, I wouldn't have achieved what I have if I'd settled down in Spain. Letting go is part of moving on. And the lure of big waves was still tugging at me.

Patience

When the Spanish sailing season ended I made my way north to a little town called Mundaka. This town is famous for its perfect, predictable left-hand wave that sometimes, with the right conditions, becomes a truly *great* wave.

The Mundaka barrel comes funnelling down the point like a high-speed locomotive on steroids. These big swells march in from the Bay of Biscay, host to some of the best waves in Europe and some of the legends of surfing, too. There are incredible tubes there, and I wanted to carve my name all over their beautiful emerald walls.

I spent a few weeks waiting and hoping for the waves to break and turn on, but they didn't. I kept picturing these perfect left-hand barrels, just like I had seen in the magazines and in my dreams, but no such luck. Mundaka was beautiful, a sleepy little fishing village with medieval architecture and old Basque cultural traditions. It was set on a river, which ran out next to the town into the sea, giving the wave its amazing shape and form. Except while I was there you would never have guessed there was *ever* a wave. The water was calm and tranquil, with not a ripple to be seen. I actually had to check I was in the right place, it was so flat.

By the second week I was starting to run out of money, patience and time. I tried to work at one of the backpackers' lodges, but that didn't last long – they wanted me to sell marijuana to the tourists, which didn't sit well with me, even though I was getting pretty desperate and knew I'd have to leave soon. I ended up sleeping in a local farmer's vegetable garden for a couple of nights, and helping myself to some of his vegetables while I was at it. That ended with a blast from his shotgun early one morning, which quickly cleared this African hobo from his beloved vegetable patch!

After 15 days and no sign of the famous wave, it was time to leave the idyllic little town or risk being stranded with no money all over again. I woke before dawn, packed up all my gear and walked to the train station, feeling frustrated, disappointed and disillusioned. I had done everything right. I had arrived there at the right time of the year and stayed for over two weeks. I had lived beyond my last dime. I couldn't believe that it wasn't to be.

It was a beautiful, crisp, cold morning; the air was gentle and calm. On the way to the station I thought I'd take a small detour to do one last surf check.

As I walked down the little cobbled street in the early-morning quiet, with the sun yet to sneak over the horizon, I heard a low grumbling sound. My heart skipped a beat. Could it be? No, surely I was hearing things. It sounded just like waves breaking. I broke into a jog and soon I was in a full-tilt sprint, my backpack banging on my shoulders. Just as the sun was rising, I reached the harbour wall and came to a panting stop. The new rays lit up the most perfect, pristine and glassy walls reeling and spinning sweetly down the point. Mundaka was on, alive and pumping in the early-morning light, and she looked beautiful.

I suited up as quickly as I could, ditched my travel bag in the branches of a nearby tree and jumped off the side of the harbour wall. It was surreal paddling out there, the light dancing off the water like a moving oil painting. It was magic. I was immersed in my dream, except it was real. Better than real, because I was the first and only one out. It was simply perfect!

I spent the morning surfing one of the fastest waves on the

planet, with a big grin on my face. I knew I had done my time. I'd been patient and kept my hope alive right up until the very last moment. It's amazing how often the universe rewards patience when you never give in and never give up hope.

Castaway

Like many young South Africans, I spent some time working in London. For one thing, it gave me a much better base from which to travel. While I was working in the city I heard about an island called Lobos, just off Fuerteventura in the Canary Islands.

I was told it had nothing except a perfect, right-hand point break all the way down one side of the island. Lobos became my next goal, and as city life was grinding, I just couldn't wait until I had sufficient cash to make the trip. I worked out that if I bought a tent so that I wouldn't have to worry about accommodation, I could live on exactly three cans of tuna, three bread rolls and two litres of water a day. I worked out a budget so that by living that way, I could probably stay for 12 days.

I arrived at Fuerte solo as always. It took me a while to work out that none of the taxis or busses will collect you if you have a surfboard. It took me hours to hike to the north end of the island where the waves were. Along the way I bought my rations, and then set up camp a kilometre away from a bakery, in the dunes, where I could get my daily bread rolls each morning. I spent the rest of my first day surfing one of the local spots called "the Bubble".

I had an epic time there for a couple of days, until the day before I was due to head to the deserted island of Lobos. On catching my last wave, I got hammered on the inside section, fell and got pushed to the bottom and sliced on the razor-sharp reef. That wasn't the worst part; as I pushed to the surface, my leash got caught around a sharp piece of reef and wouldn't let me get to the surface. My face was literally six inches away, but I just couldn't take a breath. The current was ferocious and I had to control myself and calm my mind to keep from panicking. I bent down, ripped the leash off my ankle and scrambled to the surface to get a breath.

Due to the power of the current, it took me the next half an hour to get back to my board, which was still caught on the reef underwater. It was a timely reminder to never underestimate the power of the ocean, whether the waves are big or small.

The next morning the swell looked like it was going to be on the up and Lobos could work, so I caught the ferry across the 10-kilometre channel to the island of my dreams. When we arrived I could see the waves spinning down the point from miles away; I was so excited I could hardly contain myself. I jumped off the ferry with my backpack, board and gear, and was off. The island itself is deserted, arid and very dry, with no buildings, houses or shops, just a few stray sheep and goats. Most people don't stay for long; they just walk around and jump back on the ferry and head back to Fuerte the same day. That was fine by me. I was going to surf my brains out, watch the ferry disappear, stay the night in my little tent with my rations and have the waves all to myself the following morning. I would take the ferry back the next afternoon. At least, that was the plan.

I ended up having great waves all day, just as I had hoped. A handful of Spanish surfers were there with me until late afternoon, when they jumped back on their boat, which was anchored in the bay, and headed back to Fuerteventura. I surfed late into the afternoon on my own, these perfect, solo, spinning right-hand barrels reeling down the point; it was priceless.

An hour before dark I got out, returned to where I'd stashed my gear and started setting up camp for the night. I chose a hidden nook around the corner from the point, just to get some protection

in case the wind picked up. I made a little fire and settled in for the evening, feeling happy, exhausted and content. I was also more than a little proud of myself that I had outsmarted the rest of the world and would have these perfect waves all to myself the next morning, before the ferry arrived at 10 a.m.

The night went as planned, but I woke up in the morning to a dark and ominous sky, a strong wind and a very stormy sea. I was pretty disappointed that I wasn't going to get decent waves, but I thought, No *problem, I'll just have a little morning coffee off my fire, pack up my stuff and get a lift back on the ferry when it arrives a little later.*

The time for the ferry came and went with no sign of the boat. The weather started getting dramatically worse, and then it struck me – *shit, maybe the ferry doesn't come if the weather's bad!*

Little did I know that a massive storm was heading my way. And when the storms come, the ferries don't operate. So now I was stranded on the island, running low on food and water, about to weather a major storm in my little tent.

On the second day I went out to search for some more firewood, and while I was gone my tent got hit by a huge gust of wind and was literally picked up and blown out to sea. I scrambled around the island trying to find some shelter and eventually discovered a little stone enclave, used to protect goats from the storms.

This open rock shelter became my new home. I strapped my pocketknife to a stick and attempted to spear fish in the lagoon, like some kind of castaway or *Survivor* contestant. I became ravenous, scavenging like Robinson Crusoe in the pelting rain, howling wind and cold night air. By the third day I was literally starving.

When the storm finally broke, on the third day, the ferry returned. I must have looked like some deranged island freak as I boarded it. I remember grabbing a packet of biscuits from one of the startled

passengers and guzzling them down. They were either very generous or too scared of this famished stranger to fight him off!

In life, if you don't plan, you plan to fail. But sometimes your
dreams don't come easy, and you get hit with a lot of obstacles
you didn't expect or plan for. When that happens, you just have to
be flexible and adaptable and go with it.

The very next day, just before I was due to head back to the UK,
I broke the leash on my surfboard. I didn't have enough money to
buy a new one, but I did have this great hat that I'd bought at the
start of the trip. It was made out of a twine-like string. So I ended
up unravelling my hat and using it to make myself a new leash for
the last two days of my trip. That made me laugh.

That trip was a massive lesson in survival on many fronts. I now
had a greater respect for reading the weather and forecasting, and
being better prepared, as well as a renewed appreciation for shelter, food and water. We so often take the simple things in life for
granted.

But I also learnt to look at a problem as a great opportunity
to find a solution – to see the opportunity in the obstacle. I was
learning just how resourceful you can be when you have to be. It
was a lesson that would stand me in good stead for what followed.

4

Hawaii

It's amazing how often we think we can just ignore our true calling in life. We push it to the back of our minds and think we can just carry on with our lives and it will eventually fade away and not faze us any more.

But if you've got big dreams, they tend to take hold of you and refuse to be ignored.

I returned to South Africa and studied marketing and sales for three years. I'd had some great experiences in Europe and the Americas, and I'd learnt a great deal about myself. I thought I would just be able to move on with the next stage of my life. But I still had one big lesson to learn: that there was no escaping my first love and true calling – surfing.

I knew that in order to truly find out how good I was, and to see if I had what it took to take on the world's best, I had to do the surfers' pilgrimage. I had to test myself against some of the biggest waves and the best surfers on the planet. There was only one place in the world that would give me the answer I was looking for: the North Shore of Hawaii.

But to do that, I needed money. I've always seen money as nothing more than a tool to get me from one goal to the next. I'm not very good at saving or investing it, but I always seem to find a way to use it to fuel my dreams. And that's always been okay with me. I might not have a big bank account, but I've built up a vault-full of amazing memories; I'm rich in dreams, and I have a healthy balance of friends, family, relationships and work. Well, most of the time – striking the work–life balance was often more tricky than I expected.

In 1999 I decided to get my skipper's ticket. I already had plenty of sailing and racing experience, but managing yacht deliveries would give me a free passage across the Atlantic from Cape Town to the Caribbean.

I arrived in the British Virgin Islands and worked cleaning boats until I found my way onto one of the race boats. With my previous racing experience I managed to secure a slot getting paid to race one of the top 40-foot race boats around the Caribbean.

What an awesome job! Sailing between different islands, racing in regattas around the Caribbean over the season – I was getting paid to live another childhood dream, which was to sail profes-sionally. It was an epic time.

At the end of the race circuit I was recommended to one of the bigger boats, and was asked to become first mate and race captain on one of the top American race boats. The *Donnybrook* was owned by the president of US Sailing himself, Jim Muldoon. It was a beautiful 72-foot carbon sled, a racing machine like no other. I was in heaven. I ended up taking the boat all over the Caribbean and back up to Annapolis in America, racing the Chesapeake series and then the prestigious Marblehead to Halifax race, from Massachusetts to Nova Scotia in Canada. I raced all the top big-boat series in Sweden, including the Gotland race. It was like a dream come true. But I knew I didn't want to do it forever.

As much as I loved sailing and racing the fastest multimillion-dollar boats in the world, I was still a surfer through and through. Hawaii was still calling, and her siren song was getting louder.

I wasn't getting any chances to surf while I was sailing, but in the last couple of months I trained as much as possible before and after work. I told myself I would just have to get fit while I was over in Hawaii. It had taken me a year of working and a decade of dreaming to get to the islands, so I was determined to stay in Hawaii for as long as my tourist visa would allow.

The pilgrimage

It was only when I flew in and saw the tiny chain of islands in the middle of the vast Pacific Ocean that I realised how remote Hawaii really is.

The Pacific's full raw energy is harnessed and captured by the islands. Hawaii is totally exposed to every drop of swell that travels across the ocean, as there is nothing to slow them down, shelter or dissipate them. This is why the waves there are so powerful, pristine and perfect. My first season on the North Shore was a serious wake-up call. It was the first time I had truly experienced the power of the Pacific, and it really packed a punch.

When the plane came in to land on the island of Oahu, I knew I was in for something truly special. Surfers the world over dream of making this pilgrimage and I was finally here. I had made it.

I first set eyes on the North Shore from the top of a rise after coming through pineapple fields. I looked down and the golden mile was revealed. It was everything I had ever imagined, and far more. Big, perfect waves rolling in all along the coastline – endless potential from the deep-blue Pacific.

The waves here are truly incredible, and it's no wonder that the whole lifestyle, absolutely everything, is based around surfing.

When I say everything, I mean *everything* revolves around the current state of the surf, the future possibility of surf, and what the waves are forecast to do over the weeks and months ahead. People here eat, breathe and sleep surfing. Whether you're a doctor, a painter or a lawyer, you're wearing board shorts, a vest and flip-flops – everybody seems to live the surf and beach lifestyle in Hawaii. It's awesome. I felt completely at home. I had finally found my tribe, a place where I fitted in.

In Hawaii you are part of a tribe of watermen with a deep affinity and love for the ocean, and for riding bigger, heavier waves. I've never experienced anything like it anywhere else in the world. The pilgrimage to the North Shore of Hawaii is truly a spiritual journey for any surfer. It's a place where you find yourself; find out what you are truly made of – and whether you have what it takes.

Waimea wake-up

Hawaii really kicks into gear when the big winter swells come marching in from deep within the Pacific. They travel for thousands of miles, uninterrupted, unaltered and pristine. Waimea is big-wave surfing heaven, and a place steeped in history. The first big waves were ridden here, conquered by pioneers of the sport like Miki Dora and Greg "Da Bull" Noll. After dreaming of riding it for so long, it was a truly magic moment when I finally tackled it.

My first session at Waimea opened my eyes to what it was going to take for me to get really good at surfing bigger waves and, more importantly, what it was going to take to survive them. It was a definite graduation.

That first big storm of the season had everyone excited. The swells started arriving late in the afternoon. I could see the bay out the front of the backpackers where I was staying, and it just started getting steadily bigger and bigger. In Hawaii the swell grows more quickly than anywhere else I have been. It can double in size from 10 feet to 25 feet within two hours, so you better be prepared. By the time I went to sleep, it was booming. I remember lying in my bed in the little dorm room, at about 11 p.m., counting the seconds between the waves breaking: 18, 19, 20 seconds ... BOOM! And then another ... BOOM! As the hours crept by the period grew, signalling the increasing power being packed into each wave as it gathered might and momentum on its journey towards the shore. A little after midnight, the waves began breaking so loudly, with such immense intensity and power, that the ground actually trembled under my bed. I couldn't sleep. I got up, closed the door quietly behind me and ran the 150 metres down to the beach.

In the moonlight the waves looked like they were breaking in slow motion. That's when you know they're really big. My sense of anticipation was matched only by an equal amount of my own fear.

I sat and watched the massive waves come thundering in and felt small and insignificant. Sounds are amplified at night, so everything feels bigger and louder than normal. And because everything else is so quiet, all you hear is the rumble. Even though this was everything I had been working towards, I started doubting myself, my ability, my fitness. I was pretty scared of what I might be facing in the morning.

I was up early – who could sleep with the ground literally shaking beneath their bed all night long? I got my two big boards ready to go. The biggest board I had was my trusty 7.10-footer, which was still about two feet shorter than the boards everyone else used for big surf. But this was what I was used to, and I was ready. At least, I thought I was.

I went down to Waimea Bay, armed and ready for battle. I hadn't spent any time analysing the spot. I just knew I had to get through the infamous Waimea Bay shore break before I could even get out there. And if you have ever watched that shore break you will

understand why so many people have drowned coming in or going out, because if you time it wrong, you are in serious trouble.

Waimea is no normal shore break – it's the scariest shore break on the planet, because it breaks in such shallow water: 15- to 20-foot waves breaking in two feet of water – that's practically directly onto the sand.

I watched and waited with a couple of the other big-wave riders as we timed our entry right between the sets and the massive surges. Regulars know that the "Keyhole", in the corner of the bay, is where it's easiest to get both in and out, but in my rush and inexperience I didn't know this yet. But, after 15 minutes of watching, I had it figured out. Just after the next set of big ones battered the shore and broke someone's board just 20 metres from the sand, I sneaked out through the Keyhole.

Within the first hour I managed to get two waves. The first was a smaller one with an air-drop; I made it, which instantly gave me more confidence than I deserved, as this was only the beginning of the day. The second was on one of the set waves, and was very different. I took off late and free-fell half of the 20-foot face, but managed to somehow reconnect with my board – amazingly.

Wow, that's unbelievable, I've got this! I thought, only to see a whole curtain of water fold over and down, just 10 feet in front of me. I'd never seen that happen before. The thundering lip of the barrel of the wave had actually thrown itself right over me and beat me over 30 feet down to the bottom while I was still riding down the face, straight towards the beach.

The outcome of this was not favourable for me at all. I got completely hammered, but at least I could see what was coming as the curtain on my show literally came down right before my eyes. After getting battered and beaten by the raw power of the Pacific, I managed to come up just in time to see my favourite board in two pieces, before another two huge waves detonated on my head.

After a great deal of swimming, I managed to get pushed into the Keyhole and somehow timed it perfectly to scramble back to the safety of land. My next dilemma was having no board to ride Waimea for the rest of the day. I was desperate; I didn't want to miss any part of this swell, so I ended up borrowing a 10-footer from a friend I had made during the first week. A board I had never tried, and two feet longer than anything I had ever used before ... but it was built for the bay and seeing that I didn't have another to ride, it seemed like a good option. Everyone else was riding them, and my experience on my skinny little 8-footer had had a horrific ending, so this would be fine, right? Wrong.

The waves just kept getting bigger. This time it took me half an hour to get a gap through the Keyhole at the shore break, which was looking more ominous and deadly with every set that came in. Eventually I managed to sneak out, and I did feel a little more comfortable being on a bigger board, even though it felt really cumbersome.

It was almost an hour before I was in the right place and position. I had waited my turn long enough to know that no one was going to give me stick for going. When the next big set started looming on the horizon, it was my turn.

There was one guy on my inside paddling for the wave, but I wasn't sure if he was going to go, so I started paddling and was suddenly in. The golden rule in big-wave surfing is that once you are in and committed, there's no going back, no matter what. *Okay*, I thought. *This is it, I'm going!*

I got to my feet and everything felt good for the first split second, until I felt the wind starting to lift the front of the board. There was a great deal more board under my feet than I was used to. I tried to push it down by shifting my weight further over my front foot, but it was already too late. The wind had me – it had

taken the nose of the board and wasn't letting it go! By the time I knew what was happening, I was upside down in mid-air, falling 20 feet. When I hit the water I didn't penetrate because I was travelling too fast. Instead, I started skipping down the face backwards, all the while looking up at 35 feet of wave. I could see the lip coming down to greet me, as the wave started sucking me back up the face, ready to throw me back over the falls again.

I took a deep breath and braced for impact. It seemed like forever before I could get to the surface and take one foamy breath of air before the next wave was on me. Gasping, I managed to collect myself after the third wave pushed me out a little into the channel on the side.

I looked over and saw only a quarter of the tail of my friend's board still attached to the leash. I tried to get onto it to paddle, but it was too small, so I tried swimming with it dragging behind me. That didn't work either – it just slowed me down like an anchor. By this time any chance I'd had to make it to the Keyhole in the corner was long gone; I had already drifted 200 metres into the centre of the main part of the beach. There was no point trying to swim against the rip that was taking me across towards the rocks. I was rapidly being pulled into the part of the bay where the shore break becomes absolutely frightening.

By this time, I didn't care. I just wanted to get in. But I didn't realise how difficult it was going to be to get in through this section of the shore break – until I decided to take a gap and go for it.

I got completely obliterated by the first wave, but it flushed me in towards the beach a notch, just enough to give me hope that I was going to be fine. I gained more ground with the next one, and just managed to touch the bottom with my feet. I sighed with relief – the worst was over. Not!

This was when it all started going very wrong. I could just feel the bottom with my toes, but I could also feel the force with which

I was getting sucked back out again, into the impact zone, with each wave. They were no longer pushing me towards the beach.

For the next five minutes I tried with all my might to get in, but I just got held in this same spin cycle with 15-foot waves pounding me relentlessly over and over again. The two lifeguards on duty would normally have tried to help, but they were busy rescuing another surfer who had fallen on the same wave as me. He'd blacked out and his body was floating towards the rocks. Meanwhile I was being sapped of every last bit of energy. I thought it was over for me.

Just when I had nothing left, a wave pushed me forward and I got some traction on the sand. I was waist-deep, and the ocean was still trying with all its might to drag me back out. When the next wave came surging in, trying to suck me back with it, I managed to hold my ground. I crawled up the beach on my hands and knees, my whole body shaking and convulsing as I threw up seawater. I didn't even make it to the high-water mark before I collapsed. I was just happy to be alive.

I learnt some valuable lessons that day. Firstly, use the right tools for the job. This was something my father always used to say. I had the wrong board to start with for those waves. Then I snapped mine and borrowed something too big for me. Going into new territory on a board I had never ridden and therefore wasn't familiar with – big mistake.

Secondly, know before you go. Know yourself, your own physical and mental abilities, strengths, limits, borders and boundaries, and how far you can push it, *before* you almost drown in a volatile and deadly environment.

Thirdly, and probably most importantly, know your environment and your surroundings. Make sure of the entry and exit points for when you get into trouble. If you don't have an exit plan in case you get into trouble, then you shouldn't be out there!

Lastly, when you lose, don't lose the lesson. What I gained and learnt from that day has probably saved my life many times over.

Big fish

In the same way that I learnt from the greats as a young surfer in Cape Town, I was introduced to the big breaks in Hawaii by some local legends. Foremost among them was Clark Abbey, a true, old-school Hawaiian big-wave rider right down to the last drop.

Clark had ancient Hawaiian waterman ancestry. He had dark skin and a serious face, and when you got to know him you discovered he also had a big heart and a massive smile. To this day, he is one of the few genuinely honest and sincere people I have ever met. He's authentic through and through.

Clark shaped his own boards for Waimea Bay. He didn't use a leash or a wetsuit; he was a purist. He stood for everything I imagined the ancient Hawaiians stood for: a pure love and understanding of the ocean, wanting to ride it in any shape or form, big or small, crazy or comfortable, and on any craft. As long as they were in the ocean, they were content. It was their home, as it was mine. I could see that Clark felt the most alive, content and free when he was in the water. It was his holy place, just as it was mine. The ocean was his church and Waimea was his sanctuary.

Every time Waimea broke, from the first time in the season to the last, Clark would be there. He never missed a swell; Clark would be out there, waiting for his beauties to arrive. He knew they would always come.

He taught me so many simple yet valuable lessons, whether he knew it or not. He also got me out of serious trouble once – but more on that later.

I met Clark a short while after that first heavy experience out at Waimea. From then on I became super focused on my training.

Here comes trouble! The three Bertish boys: me (top), Greg (bottom left) and Conn (bottom right)

On a learning curve at Eland's Bay in 1986

In 1987, with my first sponsored board by Sport Unlimited's Mark Burton Moore – stoked!

My old man, Keith, as a young surfer

The Bertish brothers surfing a big wave at Dungeons in 2006. From left to right, Conn, Greg and me

© Pierre Marqua

My amazing parents, Keith and Fran Bertish

On Saba island in the Caribbean, where I found my loyal travel buddy, the Frog

Travelling the world, taking yachts across the Atlantic

I raced professionally in the US for three years as a bowman on the 72-foot American *Donnybrook*

The Hawaiian crew of 1999: Jeff Ladove, Simon Jayham and me

The Bertish brothers on a surfing expedition in South Sumatra, Indonesia, in 2009

Surfing Backdoor pipeline for the first time. Don't panic when you panic!

My first big-wave session at Waimea – I learnt many valuable lessons that day

© Jason Murray

Todos 2000: One of my best waves ever – huge, beautiful, clean face and perfect drop

© Jason Murray

One of the most critical drops of my life at Todos – a make-or-break moment

The first documented big-wave paddle-in at Jaws, Pe'ahi, Hawaii – making history, February 2001

Stoked to be safe and alive – with Matt Kinoshida after making surfing history at Jaws

The cover story in the "Power of the Mind" edition of *ZigZag* magazine in August 2001

About to paddle to Alcatraz with my buddy Brian, 2001

The Frog and I travelling through Nepal in 2001 – pure freedom

Driving down to meet Evan Slater for an interview with *Surfer* magazine in 2001

Like him, I stopped drinking for the season. For the first month or two in Hawaii I'd just had fun, drinking, meeting girls and surfing. But that day changed everything.

Pipeline

Pipeline gave me my second big Hawaiian lesson.

The Banzai Pipeline is one of the most famous – and infamous – surfing spots in the world, let alone on the North Shore. It's a heavy, hard-breaking, dangerous left-hander that packs a mean punch. It comes in from deep water, hits the very shallow reef, jumps up and throws out into a fierce and fast barrel, over a deadly shallow coral bottom. If you've surfed Pipeline when it's big, you've normally got the scars to prove it.

And then there's Backdoor, the right-hand break off the same wave, not as perfect and even shallower. When Backdoor gets really solid, most people move across to Pipe, because it gets too scary, shallow and dangerous.

When the waves get big at Backdoor, it's not a case of *if* you're going to hit the bottom when you wipe out, but just how hard and with what part of your body. I remember taking off on a pretty solid wave about halfway through my session. It was big, and it started picking up and lurching out quicker than I expected. As I took off and got to my feet I knew I was late and I might not be able to make an angled take-off into the barrel, so I just tried to focus on making the drop by air-dropping straight down.

As I felt myself disconnect from my board I tried to stretch out while dropping weightlessly to the bottom of the wave. As the board got to the bottom, I just managed to get my body over it again. I was thinking, *I've got this, I'm going to make this drop.* I reconnected with my board, but I knew the lip would be thundering down somewhere close behind me. I just didn't realise *how*

close. It came down hard right above me and landed square on my head, literally compressing me and pile-driving me right through my board.

I went down instantly and hit the bottom really hard, cutting open my feet on impact. But at least I had hit it with my feet and not my head, which is normally good news – in theory I could just push right off the bottom and head directly up to the surface to catch another breath before the next wave thundered down on me. So I pushed off, expecting to start shooting up to the surface. That's when everything jarred, and I felt this massive jolt down my spine.

My arms and legs were paralysed for a few seconds, which is a really bad thing and absolutely frightening when you are under-water and not able to breathe. I was shocked, dazed and confused. Something was drastically wrong. But I started getting some feeling back in my arms and legs, so I put my hands up above my head and, to my absolute horror, felt solid rock. But I'd just pushed off solid rock with my feet ... now I was even more confused. I opened my eyes and saw nothing but black, bubbles and turbu-lence. I started to panic, and that's when I remembered the best piece of Hawaiian advice Clark ever gave me: "When you panic, don't panic."

In situations like this it's so important to control your emotions and your thoughts, to slow everything down and calm your mind. If you don't, you'll panic even more. This will cause your worst nightmare to become a reality, and you *will* drown. I collected myself, calmed my mind and felt to the side of me. There was rock. To the other side, more rock. The only other thing I could think of as the last remaining air started to drain out of me was to reach down and feel for my leash, which was connected to my board, which should always be near the surface.

Taut as a guitar string, it was pulling out slightly to my left.

Aware that if it snapped I would lose my last link to the surface, I very carefully followed it using my hands to lead me up and out. That's when I realised that I'd been pushed down through a small hole in the rocks, straight into an underwater cave.

I followed the leash hand over hand, up and out of the hole, which was literally a metre wide. I scrambled to the surface just in time to take a breath before the next wave got me. It pushed me back down and bounced me along the bottom, the rock cutting open my elbow and forearm. But it also flushed me towards the shore, and within a minute I had washed up onto the beach.

Without a doubt, that was one of the scariest experiences of my life. But because I was able to keep my head, I survived. That situation brought home how important it is to know your environment, to know what you are getting into and to plan properly.

It was also a timely reminder that I was not invincible; that sometimes things are out of your control and you need to remain calm, be able to slow things down and make quick, rational decisions under pressure in order to survive. I'm not one for tattoos, even though the reef at Pipeline left me with a couple of new scars, but there's one motto that is now forever inked in my mind: When you panic, don't panic!

Possibles

Even the best planning can leave you stranded. The ocean is a mistress who likes nothing more than to be unpredictable.

At Waimea Bay there is a pretty good short left that breaks off the main peak, so you can surf the wave left, instead of the usual right. But not many people do, because the left takes you straight into the edge of an enclosed rocky bay with a really nasty reef that sticks out of the water and no real exit. So if you do go left when it's big and you don't make it, or get caught inside by the next one,

you can get yourself into a whole world of trouble. I had been left a few times and managed to make it out in one piece, so I started to think I was pretty cool. But the ocean has a way of keeping you humble.

The wave just on the other side of this left, off Waimea, is a right-hander that breaks into a little cove. It's called Impossibles, and for good reason – most people are convinced it's impossible to surf. I think there are only one or two people who have ever managed to surf it. If you get stuck in there, there really is no way out. There's a low, rocky cliff face all around the cove and a jagged reef on the other side, so you just get stuck in the cauldron of the impact zone. The only way to not get smashed against the cliff face if you get caught in there is to stay in the impact zone until after the set has moved through, which is exactly where you don't want to be.

That didn't deter me, though. I remember watching the break one day and thinking, *I'm going to rename this place "Possibles"!*

I had been watching and studying the swell, and I started to believe that as long as I didn't take off on the first or second wave of the set, I would be fine. I was super fit, well trained, ready, and really cocky. I was at my physical peak and felt invincible. It's a scary state of mind – you're so oozing with confidence, you believe you can literally do anything.

I remember taking off on the third wave of the set. I managed to make the late drop, slide into the barrel and ride as far as I could, and I actually almost made it out, but then I got clipped trying to come through as I pulled off the back of the wave. I looked up and that's when I saw another four or five waves stacked up waiting to unload directly onto my head – all of them with faces in excess of 20 feet.

Normally you have three or four waves in a set, but this was an unusually long long-period swell. It was a monster set. To this day I've never seen so many waves in a set. They just kept coming at me, one after the other. I counted at least 10 waves before I lost count and started being more concerned about how I was going to get out of the situation. It was quickly becoming a problem. I had to keep swimming back into the impact zone to prevent getting washed onto the rocks and into the cliff face, but I was starting to tire from being continually smashed by the waves. I was running out of energy and losing strength fast, and I realised that if I stayed there for another four or five waves, I was going to drown. I had to make a call.

As far as I could see, the only way out was to try to get flushed under the rock ledge, between Impossibles and the Waimea left, through an underwater cave and out the other side into the bay. I had to give it a try. I took off my leash so I wouldn't get pinned by my board and went with the surge as it sucked me under the ledge and then through the cave. Bouncing off the sides, I went with the current and the turbulence, until I came out the other side. I just missed the rocks and ended up being flushed into the inside impact zone of Waimea Bay. As the old saying goes, "Out of the frying pan and into the fire" – just add a whole lot of wild water. Still, it was a relief to be back in "familiar" territory.

Getting flushed through and around that rock ledge was a harrowing experience. It was another important reminder that you are never invincible in the ocean. The ocean always rules supreme and nature always finds a way to keep you grounded and humble.

I couldn't have predicted that the set I chose to tame would be the longest I'd ever encountered. But that's the thing about the ocean – she does what she feels like and doesn't give a damn about our plans. If I hadn't been as physically fit and prepared as I was, I never would have made it.

I came very close to paying the ultimate price that day. One thing I've learnt is that when things go wrong in the ocean, they go horribly wrong. That's when you'd better make sure you are as prepared as you ever can be.

Earn it!

Of course, I went back for more. But this time it wasn't what was happening under the water that was scary, it was the vibe on top of it.

You can go to Hawaii like so many starry-eyed young surfers and try to live the dream, but if you're cocky and arrogant, rather than humble and respectful, take heed – you may end up getting a rude awakening, learning the hard way or being sent home early, either beaten up or in a box.

North Shore locals don't enjoy the constant stream of *haole* (pronounced "how-lee", it basically means non-Hawaiian) surfers that invade their territory every winter, hungry to take as many waves as they can, chase the glory and become the next surf hero, the next cover star of *Surfer* magazine. It seems like everyone is trying to make a name for themselves out there, and it's a dog-eat-dog vibe in the water. Watching from land with the naked eye you don't notice it, but it's a whole other world when you're out there. Very few people know it exists, but it's not pretty and it's not pleasant. It's really heavy out there, and super intense.

I've seen guys come to Hawaii with all the kit, looking like they've just stepped out of some surfing magazine, and they never even get into the water. Others talk the talk, go out there and never get a wave. They talk a great game, but once they get into the powerful surf of the North Pacific, it's a different story. In Hawaii, there's no bullshitting anyone, including yourself. The ocean here will humble you and put you in your place very quickly. And if she doesn't, believe me, the heavy locals definitely will.

A couple of weeks after recovering from my Waimea Bay wake-up call, I was surfing Backdoor, where the locals are intense and super protective of their waves. The heavies here are renowned, revered and feared. They are known as Da Hui – the Black Shorts – and no matter what, you don't create any issues with these guys or your time on the North Shore is done. I mean instantly over, as in get on a plane as quickly as you can and get out of there.

You just need to make one rookie error, drop in on a local "Hui" who's having a bad day, and you're going to run into trouble. Just do your best to stay out of their way. Don't even paddle for a wave they are looking at or it's probably going to go horribly wrong for you out there.

On this day, I'd only been out for half an hour. The pack of people surfing Backdoor was thick and the atmosphere in the water was so tense you could almost taste it. You could smell the fear. To make matters worse, there hadn't been a swell in a while, so the pack was like a bunch of rabid dogs, fighting for everything – even the rivalry between the usual heavies was worse than normal.

I'd had one wave already when the next set started lining up. I let the first two waves go, as some of the other guys had the inside line, and I tried to be patient and not get into any trouble. But the third one looked good. I saw one of the other guys starting to paddle far on my inside, but I knew he was too deep and would probably pull out at the last second, since there was no way he was going to make it.

So I engaged, committed and caught it. As I got to my feet, I looked back and saw that the other guy had gone, too. He was up, and even though he was too deep, he was still going. I tried to pull out off the wave, but it was too late; I did manage to pull off the top, but the section still came down on him, inside the barrel, and that's when I knew what was coming. If this was one of the locals, which I had a feeling it was, I was going to be in deep shit when he

came up – even though he wouldn't have made that wave regardless of me being there or not.

Unfortunately, he turned out to be one of the heavier locals. I sat up on my board and waited for him, gave him a heads-up as he paddled back out, and then began to apologise. And that's where it all started going wrong.

"Where the fuck you from, bra? I don't see you here before. And if I don't see you here, you don't live here and if I don't know you, you don't come surf here. I think you go surf somewhere else."

The thing is, I'm not very good at being told to get out of the water. I'm courteous and respectful, but I believe the ocean is for everyone. More than that, it's my church. But in Hawaii, and especially on North Shore, it really doesn't work that way. It's more like "their way or the highway" – or risk getting your face smashed in by five locals and ending up in hospital or on a plane home, or both.

So I apologised again and paddled away, and went and sat on the shoulder of the break for a while. Half an hour later the same guy was paddling back from being dropped in on by some other guy. He was shouting and swearing, and then he sees me still in the water and starts going mental.

"Hey, *haole* boy! Don't you listen? I thought I told you to get out the fucking water, bra?"

I told him I wasn't getting in anyone's way or interfering, and that I would move down the beach, but I wasn't getting out of the water; the ocean is for everyone to share. He carried on shouting at me and started spraying water in my face, and when I didn't back down he paddled back into the line-up and had words with some of the other big boys out there. Now you don't want to mess with the whole crew, that's just suicidal. So I lay down on my board and started paddling down the beach before things got really bad.

Guys get beaten up in the water here all the time. That's not what I was out there for.

I could hear them shouting at me as I paddled away, but I wasn't going to look back and make eye contact. I wanted to stay on the North Shore for the next month or two, and I really didn't need a Hui's "black mark" on my name – if that happens, your season is pretty much over, forever. Pack your bags and get on a flight home.

The next day I took my bike to check the surf and by sheer misfortune, who should be in the car park but my Hui mate from the day before! He recognised me instantly and called over two of his friends. They surrounded me in the car park and said they'd beat the crap out of me if I didn't leave the island immediately. I stood my ground, then ducked as one took a swing at me. (You don't want to try to punch one of these guys back, otherwise you're done.) The others started picking up stones and throwing them at me. I just turned and cycled away, dodging the stones, while they shouted after me, "You better leave the island, *haole*, 'cause if we see you out here again, you gonna get fucked up!"

I had this horrible, uncomfortable feeling all day. I knew that if I got into trouble with the Hui it would be game over. And I had worked so hard to get here. For the first time in my life I actually thought of shaving my head to disguise myself. I really didn't want to have to leave Hawaii, but I also didn't want to have to be concerned about getting beaten up every time I got into the water.

So I just tried to lie low for the next couple of weeks, surfing further down the golden mile, away from the heavies. I kept to Pinballs and some other spots on the other side of the island. Three weeks after the incident I was still feeling pretty nervous when a huge swell hit and Waimea Bay lit up with perfect, clean 30- to 40-foot face waves. It was a beautiful day for the bay.

I headed out with Clark Abbey and we surfed these big, beautiful waves all morning. On one of the biggest sets of the day I

managed to be in the *perfect* spot; I put my head down and gave it everything, and I was in. I dropped in super deep and later than anyone else. Two other surfers got eaten by the foam and white water as it exploded behind us, but I managed to hold on until the white water subsided enough at the end, before pulling out into the channel right next to – you guessed it – the Hui local I had had the altercation with and one of his heavy friends!

He looked like he was about to say something when Clark paddled up to me with a big smile. "Nice wave, Chris," he said. "That was a heavy drop!" The heavy looked at me long and hard, then looked at Clark and then back at me, and just nodded his head in a heads-up gesture. I knew it was his way of saying, "Hey! Respect! Nice wave. You not just some *haole*, coming to steal our ripper waves. You're legit, and that heavy drop on one of the biggest sets of the day just earned you our respect."

No words were exchanged; none were necessary. Just a common understanding that broke the curse and earned me the right to stay. I wouldn't be stupid enough to blow it again; there are no second chances there.

In Hawaii you have to really push yourself and dig deep to earn respect, not only from others, but also from within yourself. With that one wave I had earned my stripes and my place in the line-up at any of the heavy-wave spots. I wasn't just some tourist looking to live the dream and hustle a few small waves from the locals, steal their girls and go back home saying I had surfed the North Shore. I was a big-wave surfer and fast becoming a waterman.

Respect isn't given there, it's earned. That's the Hawaiian way, and that's what the North Shore is all about.

5

The Big Four

Regrouping

That first season in Hawaii made me realise that I was pretty good. But if I wanted to be *really* good, as good as the best, or even better than the best, I would have to make some dramatic changes.

Everything had started coming into focus in terms of my attitude, equipment, goals, training and all the immense preparation required, both physical and mental, to do what I wanted to do with my life. My reason for being, my "why", my purpose, was becoming clear.

What was also clear was that it would take courage, hard work and sacrifice if I was to continue to evolve, to get better, wiser and stronger, and be able to go the distance. Hawaii really focused my mind on becoming the best big-wave surfer I could be. I had my mission, and I was prepared to do anything to achieve it.

That first trip to Hawaii also made me realise that I was part of something so much bigger than I'd initially thought. If your goal takes you out of the mainstream, you can often feel like you're the only person in the world chasing a dream. It can get pretty lonely at times. But that first season in Hawaii showed me that there were others like me, determined to ride these big ocean beasts. It made me feel a whole lot more connected. I was part of this

amazing and unique tribe of people who had the same love and passion for big waves, who shared a connection with the ocean. We were all big-wave warriors prepared to sacrifice everything, to leave everything behind, to do whatever it took, whenever, in order to be there to greet those massive monsters when they arose each winter from out of the deep.

I travelled back to South Africa via Nepal, a place I'd always wanted to visit. It's about as far away from the comfort zone of the ocean – my particular church and sanctuary – as one can get, but somehow it's the only other place on the planet where I've felt the same connection with nature, the same immense sense of serenity, peacefulness and tranquillity. In the Himalayas my mind was calm, still and as crisp and clear as the high mountain air.

Besides a couple of scary Nepalese bus rides, I spent heart-stilling days in complete silence, trekking barefoot and solo up into the mountains near Pokhara. Just me and my backpack, packed with a warm yak-wool jersey from the local village, a couple of cans of tuna and some bottled water. A lot of people are uncomfort-able being alone for extended periods of time, but I enjoyed the solitude of that trip. To be alone and silent, high up in the pure mountain air, free from the clutter and noise of the city is good for the soul.

On the long bus ride up into the mountains I met an old man who left a big impression. He possessed true wisdom and reminded me that the important things in life are often the simplest. In that environment you realise that life is not about the material stuff many strive to earn and accumulate. Life – in its simplest essence, in its truest, most beautiful form – is all about simplicity; true wealth is being content within yourself.

It's amazing that two such starkly different environments – the ocean and the mountains – have taught me life's simple truths. Nature is the true guru, the teacher of all things, abundant in examples and wisdom. Most of us are just too busy, our lives too cluttered, to really stop and listen. We can draw so much energy from her; all we have to do is remind ourselves to slow down, breathe, take it all in, let it all out and let go. Nature keeps us grounded, humble and truly connected. Luckily, it's one of the few things in life that is still free. Embrace it, use it, protect it and respect it.

Nepal was the perfect place for me to gather my thoughts and plan for the next big challenge in my life.

Mission possible

I was at a crossroads: discover just how good I could become as a big-wave surfer, or move on, settle down, get a job and never know the answer to that question.

Something in me kept driving me back to the ocean, to bigger and bigger waves. I realised I just couldn't ignore the calling any more. To see how good I was, I had to test myself against the best. I had to find the biggest waves on earth and try to surf them. It was going to cost me everything I had, and there would be times when it would demand even more. But I knew that doing this would end up teaching me everything I needed to know about life; about myself and about dealing with setbacks, overcoming obstacles, facing my fears and achieving my goals and dreams.

After months of research and soul-searching, I narrowed it down to the four biggest, heaviest and scariest waves on earth: Waimea, Todos Santos, Teahupoo and Mavericks. Each one of these belongs in the big-wave surfing Hall of Fame.

I had already experienced Waimea, in its day the most famous surfing spot on Hawaii's North Shore and, some would argue, in the world. Waimea is where it all began, a place where legends were born. The greats of big-wave surfing all made their names

there, including the legendary Hawaiian waterman Eddie Aikau. For years it had been a place exclusively for local surfers. Many outsiders who knew about it didn't want to surf there; there's an ancient temple and burial ground overlooking the bay, and there were stories of human sacrifices and rumours that the bay was cursed. A few accidents by surfers who ventured there confirmed these superstitions. But in 1957, Californian Greg Noll went over and surfed it a couple of times when it was big, survived and shattered the myth. This instantly opened up the bay to a wider audience.

Isla Todos Santos is a tiny isolated island located 30 kilometres off the north coast of Mexico, and its waves are big, dangerous and fast. The most famous break here is called "Killers" and it can easily get up to 65 feet. The wave was discovered in the sixties and it is one of the premier big-wave surf spots in the world today.

Teahupoo (popularly pronounced as "cho-pu") lies in a south-west corner of Tahiti. The wave rises between two dormant volcanoes and catches the swell whipped up by the strong westerly winds known as the Roaring Forties. With no landmass within thousands of miles of the South Pacific to slow it down, when the swell hits the shallow coral shelf between Teahupoo's volcanoes, it creates a very serious, thick, powerful and terrifying wave.

And then there's Mavericks – the pinnacle, the king pin, the ultimate test. This wave, located south of San Francisco, just off a place called Half Moon Bay in Northern California, would end up challenging me and defining me as a person and a big-wave surfer more than any of the others.

They are all very different waves, but they are known worldwide as the biggest and heaviest waves on the planet. I felt that if I could give myself a shot at taking on each of these waves, then I'd really know if I had what it took to be one of the world's best big-wave surfers.

One by one, each of these waves would teach me the true meaning of unwavering focus, would test my commitment and determination, and offer a pay-off for pure perseverance. And, every so often, they would give me the beating of my life!

Close call

I started preparing for my Big Four journey in 2000. Once I had made the decision, all my focus turned to raising the funds to travel to those waves, and getting my body and mind in the right kind of shape to tackle them before I got there.

I decided that I would take a yacht over to the Caribbean and find another sailing job there. I reckoned that if I worked the full eight-month season, I would be able to save up enough money to do the trip and, for the time I was there, not have to worry about money at all. If I timed it right, I would be able to get to all four waves over a period of eight weeks, focus 100 per cent on surfing big waves while there, and tick them all off my bucket list.

But a few adventures awaited me first, and one very close call that could have changed my life's trajectory completely – and not in a good way.

I took a yacht over to the Caribbean from South Africa and another from there to Fort Lauderdale, via Bermuda Island. Then I found some day work in Florida digging trenches while I waited for another job in the Caribbean to come through.

I was busy digging when I received a phone call inviting me to work as the first mate on a big, luxury 65-foot catamaran in the Caribbean, departing immediately. So I went to the shift boss and asked him to pay me out. He had no money for me and suggested I take payment in the form of marijuana, which was a bit of a problem since I don't smoke or do drugs at all! He said it was that or nothing, but that he would come back later in the day after he'd dropped off the other staff and swap it back for money. Since I didn't have any other option, I accepted the offer. But when the time came for me to fly out, he still hadn't arrived. And I was in such a rush to get to the airport that I totally forgot about the marijuana in my cargo shorts, which I had packed into my bag.

I only remembered it again mid-air, when the announcement came over the plane's PA system: "We are about to begin our descent into Puerto Rico, en route to the British Virgin Islands. Please note that this is a zero-tolerance drug-free zone. Anyone caught with narcotics will receive the maximum punishment under Puerto Rican law." A chill ran down my spine and I started to sweat as it hit me: I still had the bankie of marijuana in my bag.

The more I ran through the situation in my head, the worse it played out, and I realised there was no way around this one. What was I going to tell customs? "Sorry, sir, I've been working illegally in America and I got paid in drugs. Now I'm smuggling those drugs to the Caribbean, where I'll also be working illegally." No matter how I tried to reason it out, I was screwed.

I kept thinking about how typical this was. I had only tried marijuana twice in my entire life and had never gone near any other drug, and now I was going to get bust in America for drug smuggling, with zero intention of doing so! My friends and family back home would hear the news that I was caught with drugs. They would know that that's not who I am at all, but everyone else would just assume, "Oh, typical surfer caught trying to make a buck smuggling drugs." My life from that point on would never be the same.

It's scary to realise how quickly one situation can change your life forever. But sometimes you just have to suck it up, accept the consequences that might be coming your way, and not think about how other people are going to react or judge you. Blaming someone else was not going to help; it was still completely my fault.

When we landed, my worst fears became a reality – there were sniffer dogs at the airport baggage carousel. I could see the sign for the toilets, and I waited for the right time and grabbed my bag. I was heading towards the toilet when one of the policemen and his sniffer dog turned from the carousel and started heading straight towards me. I tried not to panic as they got to within 15 metres, but then the dog suddenly stopped at a lady right in front of me and sat down. It was distracted for a split second; just the moment I needed to get straight past them.

It gave me time to get to the restroom, unzip my bag, fish out the bankie and flush it down the toilet. It was one of the most frightening moments of my life and a mistake I will never make again.

I made it down to the British Virgin Islands, albeit a little flustered and shaken, and got the job as first mate on the beautiful 65-foot, high-end charter catamaran named *Shangri-La*. I spent the full season taking top-end charters around the BVI area of the Caribbean, sneaking off to sail in the race circuit when the big race boats came to town.

Preparation

Cruising involved long 12- to 14-hour days and hard work, but I still managed to fit in a rigorous training schedule. I would wake up super early at 5:30 a.m., fill my backpack with running shoes, shorts, shirt and goggles, jump off the side of the boat and paddle on my surfboard to the nearest island from wherever we were anchored that day. I'd have a good 8- to 10-kilometre run, get into my swim gear and do 40 minutes of underwater and swim training, then pack my gear back into my backpack, paddle back to the boat and start my workday. I'd often repeat this at the end of each day, too. That was my routine for six days a week – I took one rest day to give my body time to recover.

Because I wasn't around surf and wasn't able to surf at all over this period, I started thinking about how I could mimic what would happen in big surf when I got caught inside by a set of at least four to five big waves. It became a fascination. I developed more and more exercises that replicated the sensation of falling and having to hold my breath, while using energy and oxygen, and these became part of my daily training regime. I was determined to give myself the edge and ensure that I was fully prepared for the challenge ahead – even more so as I wasn't able to get in any actual surf time. I was going to be ready, no excuses and no regrets.

People always find 10 reasons why they can't do something, but all you need to do is find one reason why you can, and then focus on it and just go out there and do it. There is something magical about that kind of singular focus. I was working a 12-hour day, six days a week, but I didn't look for excuses why I couldn't; I only looked for opportunities and solutions, and a way to find a path that would help me reach my goal.

Companions

Tess and Richard were my crew on the *Shangri-La* and we became a great little team. After working six, sometimes seven days a week, week after week, on back-to-back charters for three months, we had a couple of days off. We decided to stop off at a seldom-visited island called Saba on the way back from the BVI.

Because the anchorage and access to Saba make it difficult to land there, the island is untouched by the usual tourism market. Those who venture there are stunned by the island's quaint, pictur-esque beauty. The village can be seen perched 800 metres up on the side of a volcano, overlooking the Caribbean Sea (when it isn't shrouded in mist and cloud). That day, through a break in the clouds, I spotted a beach and was determined to walk to it before I left the island. It was a little hidden gem, secluded, protected and magical.

I walked along the beach with not a soul around and felt like I had been beamed back in time, until something reflective caught my eye. I walked over and peered into the foliage. Behind an overgrown bush was a copper plaque, embedded in stone. When I read the words engraved on it, they resonated deep within me:

> I walked along the evening sea and dreamed a dream that could not be. The waves that crashed upon the shore said only, dreamer, dream no more ...

I found out later that it was from a poem called "Ebb and Flow" written by a nineteenth-century American named George William Curtis, an explorer who had found his paradise. It made me realise that paradise is often closer than we think – even right under our noses.

I'm not one for stuffed toy animals, but I bought a little Saba-island tree frog, which became my faithful travel buddy. For the next 10 years he travelled everywhere with me, across oceans and to countries the world over, reminding me to always appreciate the beauty around me and all life's little blessings. Life is not only about the destination; the journey is just as important.

That winter, on the way to Trinidad to get the yacht refurbished while we hid from hurricane season, we stopped over at an amazing little island called Tobago. It might be the most beautiful island on the planet; lush, thick, green jungle forest, pristine-white sandy beaches, overhanging palm trees almost touching the water.

Anchoring off the corner of a deserted bay, I spotted an incredible little wave breaking outside, off the point of the island, but it looked pretty small and far out.

Once I'd finished all my chores, I jumped into my board shorts, grabbed my board from the cabin and paddled across to the island. I ran all the way to the end of the island to the furthest point I could see, past the last overhanging palm tree, and started the long paddle out to the distant wave.

I had to cross a deep open-water trench, which must have taken me 25 minutes. But once I got closer to the reef, I realised the wave was just as perfect as it had looked from a distance: head high, glassy and perfect, peeling down this little outer reef of lukewarm, crystal-clear, turquoise-blue lagoon water. It was like something out of a fairy tale, and with no one else around! I grinned from ear to ear before taking off on my first wave, where I got two barrels and three turns. Whaaaattt! With not a soul around, I burst out laughing as I pulled off the back of that first incredible wave. I couldn't control the massive grin on my face as I realised I had found true paradise.

I ended up surfing that wave for about two hours. Just before dusk, as I was still trying to squeeze every last bit of daylight out of the session, I saw it. Just a quick flash out of the corner of my eye: a fin.

No matter how much time you spend in the ocean or how many sharks you see, no matter that you know they're not the vicious man-eaters they're often made out to be, there is still nothing more frightening than the sight of a fin breaking the surface and heading straight for you.

Looking down into the crystal-clear water, I saw him. A stocky bull shark coming towards me. I vividly remember his eye watching me as he went straight under my board. Then he disappeared.

I quickly got my hands and legs out of the water and up on my board, where I waited with bated breath. Was he gone? And then his dorsal fin popped back up on the other side of me, like he had done a full, long, drawn-out circle around me. He turned and started coming at me again.

He did this three times. Each time he would go straight under me. Normally if a shark, especially one as aggressive as a bull shark, circles you more than once, it means he's interested. And what usually follows interest is a little tasty sample bump or bite. I didn't want to be sampled. After the third circle, I took a couple of deep breaths to calm myself, control my fear and focus on the goal: I needed to get back to shore as quietly and as quickly as possible. No thrashing, no panicking, no freaking out – I knew that would only end in disaster.

I started taking slow, calm, casual strokes in the direction of the island in the distance. The problem was that really wide trench I had to cross. I kept thinking that the deep-water channel was where the bull shark was lurking, watching, waiting for the right moment to strike. As hard as I tried to keep my thoughts in check, I couldn't help thinking, *Here I am, stuck in the middle of nowhere and nobody knows where I am. And I'm about to be eaten alive by an inquisitive and possibly very hungry bull shark.*

But thank the Lord, it never happened. I can tell you that it was the longest 25 minutes I have ever experienced to this day. It literally felt like hours. With your mind going at a hundred miles an hour, you think that every stroke might be your last, but I just tried to remain calm and focused on the goal – the beach.

When I finally reached land, exhausted, physically and mentally drained, I found a little hut right there on the beach. An island man was sitting next to it, all *irie*, chilling under his wide-brimmed reed hat. He greeted me with a big grin on his face.

"How come nobody surfs that amazing little wave out there?" I asked him. He looked at me as if I were completely crazy and then laughed, saying in his island-style accent, "No, mun, you don't want to be surfing out there, mun! You'd be crazy! That's Shark Point!"

My jaw dropped. Then it hit the floor when he walked me into the back of his hut and showed me his collection of shark jaws and teeth from Shark Point. "You lucky to still have those legs, brother," he said, never dropping the big smile on his face. "Very, very lucky."

It's one thing to be a pioneer and the first to do something. But sometimes it also pays to know exactly why nobody else has done it before. Since that day, I have learnt to get as much information as possible about a new spot or environment before I take on any new challenge. It doesn't have to change your goal, but sometimes it might change your plans – or save your life! And it will certainly make you better prepared for whatever comes your way. I've said it more than once and I'll say it again: When you lose, don't lose the lesson.

Time-travel

As the northern-hemisphere winter approached, I started strategising. I had very limited time to try to surf all of the Big Four. I didn't have the luxury of being a professional surfer, with the time and money to stay the full season. I had made enough money to stay for just two months, and I had to make them count.

I started researching and then plotting the ocean swell patterns, and noticed that they travelled west to south-east. That meant that if I was really clever and lucky, I could travel with the swell, over it, track it and follow it through and past all three of the big-wave spots, possibly on one big storm. If I got the right kind of swell in Hawaii, I could surf it there, then hop on a plane that night and catch up to it in California, after flying over it during the night from Hawaii. I could then overtake it again and meet it when it hit Northern California, surf it at Mavericks all day and then race down during the night to Mexico before it got there. Well, that was the theory anyway, and even then only *if* it was exactly the right kind of swell.

This, in itself, sounded nuts. People had spoken about it for a couple of years, surfing and tracking a single swell across the Pacific Ocean, but nobody had ever actually done it – chase a single swell between continents, islands and countries.

For me, it was all about maximising every swell and getting the most out of it. There might only be three or four major storm swells while I was over there, so I had to get my timing exactly right. I didn't want down-days to relax in between. I had to squeeze the most out of every single opportunity, because I knew I might never come back to do this again.

It meant I would have to do my own version of time-travelling, boarding planes whenever necessary and chasing swells across continents, up and down the coast in rental cars, with little to no sleep, whenever the ocean delivered storms and waves of consequence. This was my mission; whatever it would take.

I was ready. I had been training like a demon, twice a day, every day. I was fit, focused and prepared to take on anything. I finally packed up all my stuff, got on a plane and headed out to Northern California, where I had decided to set up my base. And so it began.

Mavericks

I arrived in San Francisco late in the evening. I didn't know anyone there or even where I was headed. I just knew that I had to find a little town called Half Moon Bay. How hard could that be?

It was 10 p.m. when I collected my rental car at the airport. They told me it would take about 40 minutes to get to the town. Most people didn't know anything about this mystical place called Mavericks – in December 2000, it wasn't as well known as it is today.

This was in the days before GPS, satellite navigation and Google Maps, so I grabbed a map, loaded my gear into the car and took off. After three or four hours of getting hopelessly lost all over the Bay area, I eventually found Half Moon Bay. Everything was closed up and dark, so I pulled into a small car park to try to get some sleep. I wasn't really prepared for how cold it was, even though it was mid-winter in Northern California. I'd never been there before, plus I had just come from the tropical Caribbean. I was freezing! So I pulled on my wetsuit and put on as many of my clothes as I could fit over it. I covered my hands and feet with three pairs of socks, climbed into my board bag and tried to get some sleep on the back seat of my rental car.

I woke the next morning and there was frost on the car windows. I saw a silhouette of a man walking past with a surf-board – not any ordinary surfboard, but a big-wave gun. As he walked past I cranked down the window and said, "Hey, do you know where Mavericks is?"

He said, "This is it. You're in the car park, dude. Follow this path ahead to the place of joy."

I was so excited. By a complete stroke of luck, fate or destiny, I'd found it without even knowing how. I took out my boards, which were all a great deal smaller than anything anybody else was using, as per normal. I had my wetsuit, but no boots, gloves or hood like the rest of them. But I was confident in my equipment and myself.

Most of the surfers out at Mavericks that day saw this stranger paddling out with all the wrong gear – tiny board, no booties, no gloves – and thought he was going to be the day's entertainment. There were guys on the cliffs filming Mavericks that day who later became my friends. They told me how they had laughed at me: "Hey, look at that *haole*, fresh off the boat with no booties and his tiny board!"

But when I started taking off late and deep on the sets, and making them, they started to sit up and take notice.

I won't lie: getting into the water at Mavericks that first time was very intimidating. I didn't know anyone there. I was the first South African to ride it, so it was all-new territory, and there was no one I could ask for tips about where or how. The water there is dark, freezing cold and ominous, and you've got these jagged pinnacles of rock that stick 20 feet out of the water on the inside, just waiting to greet you at the slightest miscalculation. And then you have the additional stress of getting flushed into and through the rocks if you fall, while you're being chased down by 40-foot waves – and that's just *if* you survive the hold-downs underwater when you fall.

The wave at Mavericks breaks almost two kilometres out to sea, and is so focused on the reef and so powerful that when it unloads it has twice the intensity of anything I'd ever seen or ridden. You can't imagine anything scarier. Very few people take off on the main peak, as it stands up so quickly and is so intense; 90 per cent of the daredevils sit off the side of the peak, because the wave breaks with such immense force that, either way, if you fall in the zone from that peak, you're in deep trouble. It's even scarier when you know there's no one watching your back. There's no backup, no buddy checking if you're going to be okay – it's just you!

I felt really good that I had made so much effort and focused so intensely on my training over the previous six months, because even though I hadn't surfed at all, I was super fit, confident and ready for this. This was exactly what I had been working towards. *Don't hesitate, don't doubt yourself*, I said in my pep-talk to self. *Just give it 100 per cent and go, go, go!*

I was determined to realise my dream of surfing Mavericks. I felt I'd paid my dues in Hawaii and was ready. It was time to take it up a notch, test myself, test my limits, and push my own borders and boundaries.

You shape yourself and define your own limits by constantly testing yourself, pushing yourself to the limit all the time in order to shift your comfort zone and get better and stronger. The same goes for the boards I use. It's no surprise that I was getting some pretty strange looks from the other surfers. I was using an eight-foot board, almost two feet shorter than anything else out there. Big-wave surfers overseas seemed to think I was crazy – you couldn't surf big waves on boards that small and skinny. It's suicide. You'd be looking for a board at least 9.8 to 11 feet long.

Back in South Africa, we didn't have the same boards and equipment that most of the rest of the world was using, and I had grown up riding smaller boards in bigger surf and felt comfortable on them. Yes, my relatively small, skinny boards made it far more difficult to get into waves, but once I was in, a smaller board was easier to control – even if you got in a lot later, and the drop was steeper and more vertical and, therefore, more difficult. It fitted into the wave face better and was easier to manage on a steep drop.

The other guys were on these massive boards, and if they got into a wave later, it was more difficult to negotiate the vertical drop on the longer boards. Once they had made the drop it was more difficult to turn and manoeuvre, and that's why I liked my smaller boards, because I could really *surf* those waves and not just make the drop, which was the main focus of most of the guys at that stage. That's where I had the advantage.

I wanted to take off as late, deep and critical as possible, and make it; to me, that was what testing myself was all about. That was pushing the limits. It gave me even more of a rush knowing that I was always so close to the edge, on the brink of survival; I kind of liked that. So once I was on and had made the drop, I could still surf the wave and do these amazing grab-rail, big, arcing turns on my smaller boards – it was awesome!

Sure, you need to be aware of your limitations – even more so when you arrive at a place like Mavericks. But I believe you should never let these limitations hinder you. Rather let them help guide you. Learn to get past them, through them. Whether you're limited by inferior equipment or by a physical handicap, or by growing up in a shack in poverty, use your limitations as a platform. Turn them into your foundation, on which to build and from which to launch, to become better and stronger. Your dreams are what inspire you to go beyond your limits. The only decision you have to make, the only choice, is do you have the heart to follow your dreams and the courage to make them happen?

Now when I look at the boards I used at Mavericks that first year I also think I was a little bit nuts, but I was so fit, focused and confident that I believed I could do anything – and so that's exactly what I did. What you believe, you achieve, and what you don't, you won't.

So, small boards, no booties and a ridiculously thin wetsuit – none of that made me, none of it determined what I could or could not achieve. My heart, my courage, my mind, my drive, my beliefs, my dreams – that's why I was going out there. I wanted to prove to myself, test myself. I was just about to step into my dream. I was about to surf Mavericks.

Legends

Being the first South African to surf Mavericks left an indelible imprint on my life for so many reasons, not least of which was the amazing bunch of people I got to know while surfing there. Some of them have become really close friends, others like family.

At first, the locals thought I was just some kook who had no clue what he was doing. But all that changed after I caught some big waves that first day. I only had two months over there, so I was on that wave all the time, any and every time it broke, no matter

how big or small. Mavericks literally only starts breaking at a 15-
to 20-feet face, so it's not breaking all the time, but that season
was special. It was like I was blessed; it broke most of the time
I was there.

Even when the conditions were really scary and dangerous, I
was out there. Even if it meant going out alone, in the rain, the
wind, the fog; I just wanted it with every breath. I really wanted
to learn how to surf this wave, to understand it, to be as good as
anyone else on it, so I had to maximise my time out there, to get
comfortable, familiar and confident on it.

That's what Jeff Clark, the pioneer of Mavericks, had done. He
had surfed it alone for a decade because no one could believe that
there was this massive, scary big-wave spot in Northern California.
Back then, the only known big waves were in Hawaii. So if you
weren't surfing in Hawaii, you weren't surfing big waves.

Coming from South Africa, I had read all about the legends
of Mavericks, guys like Jeff and Jay Moriarity, the rising young
superstar full of smiles, talent and aloha spirit, whose skills were
world renowned when he was in his early twenties. But I didn't
ever think or imagine I would meet these guys in person, let alone
become friends with them.

A couple of weeks after I arrived, on one of the really good, very
big days, I was out at the back, sitting really deep with a couple of
the core crew of really good surfers. A big set came in and almost
everyone scratched for the horizon. But I turned to paddle for the
wave, along with one other person. I was inside him, a little deeper
and later, and we took off together, very late, which made the drop
to the bottom very steep, vertical and critical. This surfer reached
the bottom of the wave by the skin of his teeth and I could see that
he was really stoked at the drop he'd just made.

And then he looked to the inside, 10 feet deeper, and saw me.
And I could tell by his face that he was completely baffled at the

sight of me and the fact that I was deeper and later on the wave than he was. And he had a right to be, because I only realised then that it was Jay Moriarity, one of the greatest big-wave surfers in history, one of the legends of Mavericks and someone I looked up to.

Jay was such a great person. He had this wonderfully positive, happy energy, and a love for being in the ocean and sharing that experience and magic with those around him. There are some big egos in the world of surfing, and many surfers might have been pissed off with a guy like me taking off on his inside and being so late near him, but not Jay. After his initial confusion, he just broke into this great smile and gave a huge fist-pump. He was just so happy for me, that I'd made such a late drop on such a critical wave, and even more so because I had been deeper and later than him. To get that recognition from Jay was an amazingly special moment for me.

He pulled out of the wave and shouted, "That was awesome, man! I don't know how you made that drop and where you came from, but that was awesome!" And then he asked me my name and introduced himself – as if I didn't know who he was! It's one of my most significant and special memories.

Then there was Jeff Clark. Jeff grew up watching this wave break and was the first to believe it could be ridden. He tried to get his friends to join him, but nobody wanted any part of the wave and no one believed it was legit. He ended up surfing it alone for about 10 years. It took him that long to convince anybody that there were waves of consequence outside of Hawaii, and even longer to get people to join him. When they did, it instantly opened up a whole new world.

Two of the top Hawaiians, Mark Foo and Richard Schmidt, flew over to ride this new wave in 1994. Mark ended up drowning in his first session out at Mavericks and his death sent shockwaves through the surfing community. He was one of the best big-wave surfers in the world at the time. He'd famously said: "To catch the ultimate thrill, you have to be prepared to pay the ultimate price." When he paid that price at Mavericks, it made people really take notice of the sheer size, power and magnitude of this little-known heavy-water spot.

The first time I met Jeff, I had been surfing Mavericks on a pretty scary and terrible day, one of those really dangerous days: windy, cold, dark, onshore and ominous, with some fog thrown in for good measure. This made it even more difficult to see the waves coming in from the deep and even scarier, because I was surfing it alone.

So I was out there by myself, it was starting to rain and the waves that loomed out of the mist had 30-feet faces, the sets even bigger. After almost an hour, a big set came through. It suddenly appeared out of the mist like an apparition and gave me a huge wake-up call; I realised I shouldn't be out there at all. I got really hammered and was flushed through the rocks. My board went one way around Mushroom Rock while I went the other way. I was trapped there, with tons of white water and ocean surging around me.

I was fitter, more focused and better trained than I had ever been; I was doing 300 sit-ups a day. But I realised right then and there that there's no way you can be stronger than six cubic tons of white water moving at 30 kilometres an hour against you. That's when a six-pack and supreme fitness mean nothing. I tried to reach my ankle to release myself from my leash, but there was far too much power in the ocean and I knew instantly that there was no point trying to fight it. I also knew that if my leash didn't snap pretty soon, I was going to drown ...

And that's when my leash snapped.

Until that moment, I'd thought I was invincible. But there are times when you just have to accept the power of the ocean. No matter how much control you think you have, there are some situations in life when you just have to let go – go with the flow and know that what will be, will be.

I was able to fight my way through into the inside channel. I found my board and made the long paddle in and back onto the beach. When I finally walked up the path, it was early evening. It was cold and misty and the light was fading, but in the parking lot in the distance I could just make out the stocky silhouette of a man standing in front of his truck headlights. Out of the mist he bellowed, "You, you're that crazy South African I keep hearing about. You're coming to stay with me, so you don't kill yourself."

And that was the moment I met the famous Jeff Clark.

Aloha, again

I stayed with Jeff for a week, until it looked as if a really big storm and swell would hit Hawaii in a few days. I had been tracking the storm on the charts and watching it grow and move across the Pacific. I booked a flight the next morning, packed my stuff, said my thanks and goodbyes to Jeff, and headed out to the North Shore of Oahu and Hawaii.

I arrived a couple of days before the swell, with time enough to get into the groove, and get ready and prepped before the storm slammed into the islands. I knew it was setting up to be an epic big swell, possibly the best of the season. Everyone was talking about it – the islands were alive with hype and excitement about the imminent swell. I tracked the possible trajectory of its route after hitting the islands and realised that it might be travelling in the right direction for me to be able to time-travel it, like I had planned.

The night before the swell arrived we could hear it building through the night. It was booming and the ground was already shaking as the sets broke on the outside reefs. Always a good, albeit scary, sign!

I woke up just before daybreak and headed out to Waimea. I was greeted by giant, clean, beautiful waves thundering into the bay. I spent the whole day riding them, until I literally couldn't paddle any more. I was exhausted; surfing big surf for eight hours straight takes huge amounts of concentration, energy, focus and commitment. Besides being physically demanding, it becomes a feat of mental endurance.

I got out of the water, packed my stuff into my rental car and drove the hour to the airport. As soon as I got there I booked and paid for a flight, checked in my boards and gear, and flew out at 8:30 p.m. It was a 10-hour flight, all the way across the Pacific Ocean and over the monster swell I had been riding all day in Hawaii. When I arrived in Northern California at 6 a.m., I gathered my kit and boards, collected another rental car and drove straight to the Mavericks car park at Half Moon Bay. I parked my car at 7:30 a.m., set up my equipment, got into my wetsuit and walked the 10 minutes down the path to the shore, where I would paddle out to surf the same swell I had surfed only 14 hours ago in Hawaii.

I stood on the shore for a moment, looking out at the biggest paddle-in waves I had ever seen. I didn't know it at the time, but the swell I was now chasing across the Pacific just happened to be the biggest swell of the decade. It would later become known as the big El Niño swell of 2001. The El Niño weather pattern made all the storm systems in the Pacific region even bigger and stronger that season.

The waves were massive that day, with a 22-second period – meaning there were huge amounts of deep-ocean energy within and between each wave. They had travelled a long way, stacking into each other during the 12 000-mile journey across the Pacific. They were raw, mean and breaking with a menacing amount of power and intensity, the like of which I had never seen before. I've never come across a wave that I didn't want to paddle into. But on that day, Mavericks truly frightened me. For the first time in my life I was meeting waves I didn't want any part of. Everybody was nervous out there. The waves looked purely evil and life-threateningly scary.

When the big sets came in, everybody was just trying to get out of the way. I'd always wanted to take on any wave that came my way; I'd never *not* wanted a wave because it was too big or too scary, but for the first time I had to admit that there were waves out there beyond what I considered to be "surfable". That day I witnessed waves that could not be paddled into and which I knew without a shadow of a doubt would certainly kill me if I was caught in the wrong place.

That moment changed my perception of big-wave surfing for-ever. So I played it pretty safe most of the morning, choosing wisely. I was riding my biggest board, an 8.10-footer, which was literally like a toothpick out there. Most people were on 10-foot boards or bigger that day.

A couple of hours into the session I caught the third wave of a set. I managed to free-fall into the beast and somehow negotiate the drop and the bump. But when I came around off the bottom and angled to get up into the pocket, to find the right line to give me the speed I needed to get though the inside section, I found that the two waves that had broken before it had left a lot of froth and white water on the face, which made it bumpy and hard to keep my edge as I turned up the face and held my speed. It also changed the way the wave broke, making it line up on the inside section, where it can get even scarier. Besides negotiating the bumps on the wave face, I had to contend with the white-water froth from the previous waves, and on my little board – it was just the wrong combination.

The white water started catching me from behind. I looked up to try to find an escape route, an exit point, but the wave had already lined up for the inside section; it had just hit the inside ledge and stood up even bigger than on the outside. I knew right away that I was in trouble. The wave was about to engulf me. I was about to experience the heaviest, scariest, longest hold-down and most violent beating of my life. I just hoped I would surface before I reached the jagged rocks they called "the Boneyard", and before the next wave hit me.

I took a deep breath and braced for impact. The white water engulfed me and instantly swatted me end over end. I felt myself being pushed down deeper, and at speed. I wasn't coming up at all, but I could feel I was covering a huge distance underwater – I was being dragged backwards by my one leg, as if by a giant pit bull on steroids. I tried to keep my head and hoped I wasn't going to get pushed even deeper. I needed to get to the surface before the next wave hit.

I was really battling to keep calm and hold my breath. The last bit of oxygen was running out of my system and I started struggling with frantic strokes to get to the surface. I finally broke the surface with a huge gasp, just managing to take two more quick breaths before the next wave spun me like a ragdoll and tried to rip me apart all over again. By some miracle, that one let me up pretty quickly. I had travelled almost two football fields underwater before coming up for a breath. I was just happy to have come up at all, happy to simply be alive.

Then I saw a ski coming in fast; Jeff was riding and Jay was on the back. They had seen me go down on that frothy monster and had come in to check that I was okay. They both looked very concerned. I just burst out laughing – to have these two legends coming to check on me, my heroes watching out for me! What an amazing feeling. Later they said it was one of the heaviest beatings they'd ever seen; they'd never seen someone travel that far under-water before coming up. It made me pretty happy to know I'd survived the worst hold-down of my life and was still in one piece.

There's a sad postscript to this story, though. At the end of that 2001 season, when I first met Jay Moriarity, and just as I was get-ting to know him, the surf legend met every waterman's worst fate. He was in the Maldives, doing a surf photo shoot and preparing for the big-wave season by doing his usual deep-water, free-diving training, when he had what is known as a shallow-water blackout and drowned. His death sent shockwaves through the surfing world. He was not just one of the pioneering surfers to really push the limits at Mavericks, but an amazing guy who defined the aloha spirit of pure surfing. He was one of those rare, all-round nice, happy-go-lucky guys, both in and out of the water. He is sorely missed.

Todos Santos

That afternoon, exhausted and drained from the heaviest beat-ing from the scariest waves I had surfed in my life up till that point, I went back to my rental car, got changed, packed up all my gear and checked the forecast update. It confirmed what I had suspected: the swell was going to be unmanageable and out of control at Mavericks the following day, since it was starting to swing direction and move south. Everything was going according to plan; if the swell went south, I could track it down the coast and hopefully catch it the following day in Mexico, at the third of my Big Four spots: Isla Todos Santos, an island with an infamous wave known as Killers.

Waimea, Mavericks and Todos: the perfect trifecta, all on one swell, in three consecutive days, in three different countries!

I called my friend Jeff "Snoop" Ladove in San Diego and asked him if he was planning on heading down to Mexico.

"It's looking really good for Todos tomorrow," he told me. "Chris, if you can get here in time to meet us at the border at 6 a.m., you're in!"

The El Niño swell looked like it would be hitting Mexico in the morning. The conditions could be epic. Forecasting is not an exact science and you never know what you are going to get. I could travel over a thousand miles and it might not be working at all, but there was no way I was going to miss that chance of massive waves in perfect, glassy conditions with warmer water and sunny skies! All I had to do was get there in time.

I've always believed that fortune favours the brave and those willing to take risks, those who take that leap of faith, so I got into my rental car, drove to a filling station, filled up on coffee, snacks and gas, plotted a rough route 1 300 kilometres south on my map, and hit the road.

I drove straight through the night, through Northern, Central and Southern California, only stopping every 400 kilometres or so to refuel on gas and Starbucks coffee. To this day I don't know how I managed to stay awake for 13 hours non-stop, after surfing massive waves all day to the point of exhaustion. I relied on a few trusty night-time-fatigued driving tricks: the head-out-of-the-window-at-120-kilometres-an-hour trick, the stop-every-45-minutes-and-run-around-the-car trick and the ever-faithful excessive-blinking trick. And a serious overdose of caffeine.

I also have no idea how I managed to cross the border into Mexico without a visa. I was just so jacked on coffee and a lack of sleep that crossing the border was a complete blur. I guess I just looked like one of the three American surfers I was by then travelling with.

Once through the border into Mexico, the four of us – Jeff,

Richard, Brian Caldwell and I – drove another three hours south to a tiny fishing village, where we met up with a few other big-wave surfers from San Diego. We split the cost of renting a boat from a fisherman who assured us he knew how to get out to Isla Todos Santos.

We just had to put our faith in the universe, which is difficult when you're in a little creaky fishing boat, with a skipper you've never laid eyes on before, heading out in strange foreign waters to a deep open-ocean channel, 50-foot swells and an invisible tiny island 40 kilometres out to sea.

After a couple of nail-biting hours we finally saw the island in the distance. There were massive waves breaking off the one side; they looked even taller than the island itself, and that's because they actually were!

As we rounded the side of the island we saw the wave itself: massive, glassy walls of 50-foot perfection, unloading in crystal-clear, turquoise water. It was so big and so perfect, and it looked like it was breaking in slow motion. For me, it was something out of a fairy tale. I had never, ever seen such clean, perfect big waves before. It was like I had died and been beamed into Big Wave Wonderland. After the scary, ominous waves at Mavericks the day before, this looked just like heaven!

There were only three guys in the water; everyone else was looking on hesitantly from their boats. But I couldn't get into my wetsuit and into the water quick enough. I was sleep-deprived but still running on adrenaline from the big surf at Mavericks the day before and all the caffeine from the mad, crazy drive south. After the cold, dark waves of Mavericks, these looked too good to be true. There was no doubt that the 40- to 50-foot faces out there were life-threatening – and they were predicted to get even bigger during the day – but what terrified me most was just the thought that the conditions might change before I'd had a piece of this perfection.

Coming from Cape Town, I was used to conditions being a bit more raw and wild. The big waves I grew up surfing were really rugged, so when I stood looking at the Todos that day, it just seemed magical. Everybody around me was saying, "It's too big. I think we should wait." I was looking at them like, *Are you frikkin' kidding me? It's perfect – I'm out there!*

The waves kept building, getting bigger and bigger throughout the day. But they were also so clean, breaking almost in the same place each time. I felt as if I could read them like a book, which is really unusual for a big-wave spot you've never surfed before.

I'm always interested in how people become comfortable with their environment. My American friends were used to these kinds of waves at Todos, but just not this big, whereas I came in with a completely different frame of reference. Where they saw massive waves and were hesitant, I saw something completely different after coming from the biggest, scariest, most ominous waves I had ever seen, at Mavericks, the day before.

It's an important lesson: don't let somebody else's frame of reference dictate yours. That's why I ignore anyone who tells me that something is impossible. It may be impossible for them, but that doesn't mean it's impossible for me.

Nothing is impossible, unless you believe it to be.

I waited about 10 minutes to find my place in the line-up before the first set came in. The first wave made me realise I wasn't deep enough and I let the others paddle for it while I went out another 20 feet. As I paddled over that wave I saw the next one: a huge, glassy wall of water moving towards me. I didn't hesitate at all, I didn't even blink, I just put my head down and stroked into my first Todos wave with all my might. It was big, beautiful and perfect, 40 feet of glistening Pacific power. I got into the wave late, but perfectly positioned to slip deep down the face. I was on the brink of almost disconnecting from my board, just negotiating the thundering lip, as it exploded down behind me.

It was a picture-perfect start to two of my most memorable days of surfing. By the middle of that first day, I had managed to ride at least five of the best waves of my life, as the swell continued to build. It was like a dream come true, until the biggest set of the day came in – then it all changed, in a matter of seconds.

We could see it coming from way out. It was far bigger than anything else that day. We all started scratching for the horizon and just managed to get over the first one, but the second was way bigger, and those who had let go of their boards to get through the first one were now stuck and couldn't get over the next. I had just squeaked over, so I managed to ditch my board and swim through the big one. As I tried to pick and choose the right angle at which to swim through this massive 50-foot wall of water, I realised that if I didn't get through this, if it sucked me back over, which often happens in this situation, I was in really, really deep trouble.

I just scraped through by the skin of my teeth and, luckily, when I came up on the other side there wasn't a third one coming. I was a little shaken and looked back to see a couple of the other guys who had got caught. They were littered all over the impact zone on the inside, still trying to surface and battling to get to the safety of the channel in one piece, with or without their boards. It was all about survival in those key minutes.

I realised that no matter how much training you do, it never feels like enough in these situations. When a 50-foot-plus wave catches you, no matter who you are and what you are made of, you're in trouble and you fear for your life. It's that simple. Everyone has fear; it's normal and natural. How you manage this fear, how you react to it and push through it and carry on going, is the key to success, to evolving and getting better and stronger.

That day we headed back before the sun went down, celebrating

with beers on the boat and when we reached the shore. I was utterly exhausted but stoked beyond imagination, totally and blissfully content. We went out that night and partied hard, celebrating life and the fact that we'd survived to brave another day.

Know your limits

We woke up late the following morning, trying to piece together the night before in our brains, to a sound we hadn't expected to hear: the booming of the swell as it smashed up against the outside harbour wall.

No, it couldn't be. Was it possible? The swell was still around and it sounded like it was as strong as the day before. I woke Jeff and Richard up, and we got our stuff together, trying to work out whether we could afford to hire another boat to get back out to the break and whether we were in a fit state to do so after the previous night's celebrations. "Screw it, we're here already, so, let's do it! We're in!"

We scraped our dollars together, went down to the dock and organised another boat out to the island, expecting Todos to be a great deal smaller than the day before. But we were mistaken; it was just as big and just as perfect. Sometimes the forecasts aren't always right. Luckily for us, we'd made the right call.

Once I got in the water, I realised the swell had to be peaking; it was actually stronger and possibly even bigger than the day before. My first two waves were both giants, some of the biggest set waves of the day. I air-dropped into my first wave, so late and steep that even I was surprised to make it. By mid-afternoon, I was exhausted. I was starting to cramp from fatigue, sleep deprivation and dehydration, and I knew I was pushing it.

When another of the bigger sets of the day came through, I waited till the third one, knowing it would be even bigger. I was deep, deeper than I should have been, but I had to go – even though I thought I might get barrelled. I was getting a little cocky when I stroked into this monster and started angling down the massive wall of water. About halfway down, as I was about to pull up into it, I realised it wasn't going to throw out properly and barrel, which would have allowed me to get in under the thundering lip. I was too deep to get around it, so I straightened out, and that's when I knew I was going to take a heavy beating.

Before the wave detonated me off my board, I decided to dive off headfirst. The idea was to penetrate the water, rather than hit it and skip along the surface, as so often happens in waves of this size, because you hit the water so hard and at such speed that you literally bounce. The consequences, when you are travelling at speed down the face, are horrific. And then you're still going to have to face the probability of being sucked back up and over the falls thereafter.

I braced for impact, and it hit me like a Mack truck. But it didn't just let me go; it hauled me in and held me there, drawing me up like a heavyweight wrestler heaving his opponent above his head, bracing to smash him down onto the floor. I knew I was about to get sucked back up and over the falls. It's a surfer's worst nightmare. You have no control over what happens and how you hit the water the second time around. You basically go over the top of the wave with the falling lip and get catapulted over a 50-foot precipice of water.

That means you fall from the highest point of the wave and hit the water for the second time, while trying to hold your breath, not get winded, remain calm and keep from panicking for as long as it takes to get to the surface. That is, if you don't black out.

I was thrown around underwater with such force that I felt like I was in a car accident. I got pushed so deep I could hear the boulders on the bottom rolling around like skittles; if you dive this

area, you know these boulders are each bigger than the average American car.

Normally I get to the surface by climbing up to my board using my leash, but the force was so strong that it took me ages just to reach down to my ankle. When I finally got to the end of my leash and grasped the tail of my board, I realised it was still underwater. This was a massive shock. The leash was 15 feet long and could stretch to 20 feet under waves like this. My board was almost nine feet long. So that meant I'd just been pushed close to 30 feet deep. After what felt like ages I finally broke the surface, gasped for a breath and then felt the next one on me. The second one let me up relatively quickly and I managed to get onto my board and start paddling back towards the channel. But that's when I noticed there was blood all over the front of my board.

I wasn't sure what was going on, but I had blown a couple of blood capillaries in my larynx from the pressure and the strain on my lungs, and I was coughing up blood. And I still had to get out of the impact zone. I started cramping all over and coughed up more blood. But I finally made it to the safety of the channel, and then back to the boat for a break from the madness.

Coughing up blood seems like a pretty good time to call it a day. But I felt okay and I was actually considering paddling back out. Then I stopped and thought about it. I had been pushing it for the last three days and I was still in one piece. I'd had a couple of amazing waves, probably the biggest in my life, and two really close calls. Sometimes you need to know when it's time to call it a day, when you're ahead and still alive.

There is a fine line between courage and blatant stupidity. Something's got to give eventually, and in the volatile conditions of the ocean, it isn't going to be the ocean.

I sat up on my board, in the safety of the side of the channel, and watched another big, perfect wave come thundering in on the reef. One of my friends was riding down it, hooting and howling with pure stoke and adrenaline. It made me laugh out loud. I was truly and completely stoked in every sense of the word. What an amazing four days! It really was time to be content and call it a day. And that's exactly what I did.

I had been running on adrenaline for too many hours. Now it was beginning to take its toll. If I'd pushed on, chances are I would've made a serious error in judgement that could have got me killed. My body was telling me to take a break. I knew I had to listen.

My father always told me, "In life you need to have the foresight to know where you're going, the hindsight to know where you've come from, and the insight to know when you've gone too far." Wise words that I constantly live by.

It was time to head back to California. On the drive back, the sun was setting and the sky was a fiery pastel red, filled with beautiful, raging colour. It was like the heavens were commemorating some of the best big-wave surfing ever seen.

Car-park hero

When I got back to California I had some time to reflect on what had happened over the last five days, and what I had achieved. I had done something only I had believed possible: I had actually time-travelled the swell, raced it across the Pacific Ocean, from Hawaii to California to Mexico. Not only had nobody ever done this before, but the swell I chose to chase turned out to be one of the biggest ever recorded. I didn't know it then, but my incredible journey would make it into surfing magazines and websites all over the world, and I hadn't even made it to Teahupoo yet!

The first call for an interview came just as I got back to San Francisco. It was Evan Slater, the editor of *Surfer* magazine. That

was a big moment for me; I'd grown up reading *Surfer* and really looked up to all the people it featured. Now here I was, rubbing shoulders with them, surfing these great waves with them, and they wanted to hear my story. The interview was a chance to meet Slater, a great surfer himself and a legendary editor, so I said yes without a second thought. I would never have forgiven myself for being that close and not taking advantage of such an opportunity. After all, a life filled with regret is no life at all.

"When next will you be in Santa Barbara?" Slater asked me over the phone.

"Tomorrow, I guess," I told him.

We agreed to meet in a local Starbucks at 9 a.m. the next morning. I put down the phone, got back into my rental car and drove 10 hours down to Santa Barbara for our coffee and interview. I would just have to hotfoot it back up to Northern California the same day to be back for the next big swell, which was scheduled to hit the following morning. I knew I could do it!

During the interview, Evan asked me where I was staying. I told him Half Moon Bay, near San Francisco. So he said, "No, I mean where are you staying here, in Southern Cali? Where were you staying last night when we spoke?"

And I said, "Half Moon Bay, near San Francisco."

He looked puzzled and then shocked when it dawned on him. "You mean you just drove down from San Fran last night, for this interview? No way!"

Then he chuckled. "This is going to be a great story..."

It was. Slater's story ran in the main edition of *Surfer* magazine. Under the headline "Driven", he wrote:

Since January 14, Bertish has burned through more gallons of unleaded and more kilowatts of oceanic horsepower than any surfer in the state, steamrolling back and forth between the two West Coast bullies (Mavericks and Todos Santos) like an Amtrak commuter train.

A few weeks later I was told that one of the waves I rode during those magic days at Isla Todos Santos was voted the biggest wave ridden in the world that year. As a result, I was due to win the Swell.com award, and with it $30 000 in prize money.

But something happened shortly afterwards and the prize money for the tow-in team that won the biggest wave at Cortes Bank got bumped up to $60 000, and I went from expecting to win $30 000 in prize money to being offered $100 and a gift voucher from Swell.com – which I never even received.

What's the lesson in that? Maybe that sometimes you just don't get what you deserve. I don't do what I do for money, but a little financial aid would have helped. It was a hard pill to swallow, but I refused to be bitter. The world works in mysterious ways and I believe it all comes back to you eventually, no matter how long it takes. You reap what you sow.

I may not have been financially rewarded, but I did earn some self-respect and confirmed that I was on the right path, achieving my goals and dreams, and even making a name for myself. Most importantly for me, I was proving to myself that I was as good as I thought I could be, as good as the very best. All I had needed was the opportunity.

I became something of a car-park myth. People up in Northern California told me they overheard guys talking about "this crazy guy from South Africa who was doing these crazy things". People were saying things like, "Hey, have you heard about this South African? He's surfing Mavericks on an eight-foot board." And then somebody else would say, "Yeah. He was down in Todos Santos last week and caught the biggest wave of the season there." Then someone would add, "No, it can't be the same guy! I've just seen him at Waimea in Hawaii surfing giant sets!" And then another

would pipe up, "Yeah, that's the same guy with the tiny boards and no booties; he was charging at Mavericks at the beginning of the week on that monster swell. Can it all be the same guy?"

They all wanted to know who the crazy surfer was. Because no one had heard of me; it was like I'd dropped in from another planet, disrupted the world of big-wave surfing for two months, and then disappeared. Back then, the world wasn't as digitally connected as it is now. And the community of big-wave surfers was small. There was Hawaii and California, and that was it. Now suddenly there's this stranger bouncing around in their backyard, doing crazy things, sleeping in car parks, surfing waves on tiny boards, and then disappearing again.

Another magazine article gave a rundown of the statistics of my trip. Apart from detailing technical aspects like the thickness of my wetsuit (which was way thinner than it should have been) and the fact that I lacked so many other vital pieces of equipment, they'd calculated that I'd put 5000 miles on my rental car and consumed 75 Red Bulls on the road.

Alcatraz

When you're as focused on a mission as I was in 2000, it's easy to forget about just having fun and enjoying the journey. I was training so hard, each and every day, besides when I was out surfing the big swells, that there was very little time for anything else. I wasn't in San Francisco to sightsee or party, but I did manage to take a few days off to enjoy the city.

The day after I got back from the interview with Evan Slater, I decided to go and see the famous prison of Alcatraz in San Francisco Bay. Alcatraz is such an iconic place, and I felt it would be a mistake to be staying 45 minutes from the city and not go out to see it.

But I didn't want to see Alcatraz like a tourist. And I didn't want to waste $45 on the ferry ride to get out to the island. I could do a lot with $45 at that time in my life. So I researched the tides and checked the weather forecast, and decided to use it as a training session. If I timed it right and had the right conditions, and avoided getting run over by ships and tankers, I could paddle out across the bay from Pier 39 to Alcatraz on my surfboard.

I roped in a friend, Brian Caldwell, and turned it into a mini expedition. I made sure we timed it perfectly with the currents and tides – get it wrong and you'll find yourself trying to paddle across five knots of current, which definitely won't end positively. It took us about an hour and a half. Ferries passed us, people took photos, and when we arrived at Alcatraz even the warden came down onto the pier to greet us.

"The boys were looking at you through the telescope," he said. "They told me these crazy dudes were paddling out to the island, but I just had to come and see it for myself. I've been here 25 years and nobody's ever done that before."

We had a good laugh about it.

It was yet another example of the power of positive thinking. Instead of focusing on all the reasons why you can't do something, just find one reason why you can – then focus on it, plan and make it happen. No excuses, no hesitation, no procrastination – just a choice and a decision, and then the actions that will take you in a positive direction to experience something new.

Go snow

I knew there was a storm coming in and there weren't going to be waves at Mavericks for a couple of days, as the winds were going to be wrong, but there *was* going to be snow in the mountains four hours away at Lake Tahoe. So later on that day, after getting back in from Alcatraz, I got in my car and drove from San

Francisco straight to Lake Tahoe for my next mission: learning to snowboard.

There was a three-day window before the next big swell hit and I wanted to maximise my time in between. I didn't know how to snowboard, so I rented some equipment and borrowed the rest, and climbed onto the nearest ski lift to the top of the mountain.

That's the shortened version. Here's what actually happened: I had no idea how to get off the gondola, so I just stayed on, through the various drop zones, until I reached the top of the mountain where it does a full circle and you sort of get flung off into a small pile of snow. Let's be honest, what does a South African know about ski lifts?

I picked the first and only route I could see down: it was called a "black run". Okay, so it sounded serious, but how bad could it actually be? I'd just survived five days of life-threatening 50-foot surf. I found out quickly enough, after reaching the bottom battered and bruised, not to mention a little humbled. Apparently black runs are for the most experienced skiers and snowboarders. Oops! I guess ignorance is bliss.

I fell more than a couple of times on the way down, almost hit a tree and got stuck in some really deep snow for half an hour because I went off-piste. By the time I reached the bottom, I was covered in snow from head to toe, but I could snowboard!

You never know unless you try. Sometimes you've got to throw yourself in at the deep end and learn to swim while you're drowning. I'm not able to say I'm a great snowboarder, but I guess I can make it down a black run alive, so maybe I'm not too bad.

Jaws

Three down, one to go. I planned to head out from Hawaii to Tahiti for the final leg of my Big Four project, so I packed up everything in California and headed back over to the North Shore to have a short break, catch a couple more swells and get ready for Tahiti.

It was going to be awesome. Teahupoo, the mystery wave, awaited me. At the end of two weeks of training and preparation on the North Shore, I was ready. I got to the airport, checked in and was just boarding the plane when a customs official stopped me at the gate. He looked down at my passport and back up at me and said, "Sorry, sir, did you know your visa for Tahiti expired yesterday?" I had been travelling for three months, the duration of my French visa. I had missed it by a day.

"Nooooooo!" I was so bummed out and disappointed. I asked the customs official if there was any way I could get the visa renewed.

"You could fly back to South Africa and get it renewed and fly back."

Clearly he'd never done that 52-hour flight before. It seemed my Big Four wasn't meant to be. Maybe it was fate.

I was to learn yet again that our biggest obstacles can lead to our greatest opportunities ...

By now my Big Four journey had gathered quite a following. A lot of people were tracking my progress through the web updates I was writing for Wavescape.co.za. One of them was Rick Leek, a photographer in Maui, who sent me an email the very next day. He said he'd heard what I was doing and he thought I might be the perfect guy to try to paddle into a wave called Jaws, in Maui.

He pointed out to me that the conditions that enabled you to do so were very rare, but he just wanted to find out if I might be interested, since he'd tried to entice many others and no one was keen.

And for good reason: Jaws is another world-famous big-wave

surfing spot and possibly the most famous tow-in spot (where people are towed into the wave behind a jet ski) on the planet. Most people at that time believed it was too fast, too big and too hollow to paddle into with your bare hands. Which was why Jaws wasn't part of my Big Four plan.

Jaws – or Peahi – is located on the Hawaiian island of Maui. It's where the often-controversial practice of tow-in surfing was born. Laird Hamilton made a name for himself tow-surfing Jaws. He and many others had claimed it was borderline impossible to paddle into the wave. To understand why his statement held such weight, you need to understand Laird Hamilton.

In the world of big-wave surfing, Hamilton is one of the biggest personalities. Big in the sense of what he has achieved, and big in stature and demeanour. So when Hamilton said that something could or couldn't be done, everybody listened. And according to Hamilton, Jaws was not made to be paddled.

Jaws was therefore really not part of my plan. But of course, when actually presented with the "impossible", I just couldn't help myself. Where some see obstacles, I try to see opportunities; it's a mindset, an attitude, a choice!

I told Rick I was in.

A week later he called me again, and this time he sounded super excited. "Chris, are you still keen? Because you won't believe it – next week the conditions look like they could be perfect to paddle into Jaws!"

The night before I flew out to surf Jaws for the first time, I spent hours checking and rechecking my equipment, the weather charts and my flight details. Then I lay in bed thinking about that wave, visualising what was going to happen, right down to the last detail ... Except every time I got halfway down the face of that first beautiful steep wave at Jaws – in my mind's eye – I would hit this bump, catch a rail and fall. I refused to go to sleep that night until I'd overcome the bump and could see myself making the wave. After at least 60 or 70 attempts, I finally managed to make that first steep drop at Jaws and drifted off to sleep.

Six hours later, I was up and on my way to the airport. I checked in my trusty 8.8- and 8.10-footers and boarded a jet plane to Maui. I arrived just after 6 a.m. and Rick was there to meet me with his truck, jet ski attached and ready to rock.

We headed down past Ho'okipa to the launch site at Peahi. As we turned the truck to reverse the ski into the water, it hit me: I was about to head out to try to become the first person to paddle-in surf a decent-sized wave at Jaws.

The water was crystal blue and there was a light offshore breeze – a little worrying, as wind makes it a whole lot more challenging on the take-off. It took us about 20 minutes on the ski before we came around the corner at Peahi and saw Jaws in all her glory. She peaked and glistened and roared in the early-morning sun as she broke and thundered on the reef.

Rick had managed to get a local guy, Matt Kinoshita, to come with us and also give it a try. We looked at each other. Was it possible?

While we prepped our boards and equipment, we watched the waves break and got a feeling for the sets. Finally we jumped into the water with nervous grins and much-psyched anticipation.

We paddled out alongside the channel as the beautiful blue beasts came in and broke, and marched down the reef just 50 metres off the channel next to us. I was trying to stay on Matt's inside, as I wanted to make sure I got that first wave. That's what I was there for, and the conditions looked almost perfect. The waves were big, in the 30- to 40-foot face range, but I knew if the wind picked up it would make it unnecessarily dangerous.

We saw the first set peaking on the horizon and starting to build. I managed to just sneak over the top-left corner of the wave

as it lurched out and unloaded on the reef below. The next one was bigger and I knew I wasn't going to make it over the top. I was going to have to ditch my board and try to swim through, and hope I didn't get sucked over. If I could just get through, everything would be okay.

I could feel it pulling at me, at the very fibre of my being, trying to pull both my board and me over the falls with it, but I somehow managed to get through. I quickly collected my board to get through the next one, and as I came over the third one, I saw the wave. It was exactly like I had seen it in my mind the night before, almost as if it had been taken directly from my vision. I knew instantly, this was the one! I didn't even have to process it. I swivelled, turned, put my head down and started paddling with everything I had. That was it, I was all in!

You never know unless you go. There's no such thing as failure in life, only a failure to try.

I took a couple of extra strokes to get into the wave properly, just in case. That's another one of the rules I live by in bigger surf: when you think you're in, always take two extra strokes.

I could feel the wave picking me up from behind; I was definitely in. I stood up and watched the wave unfold and get suddenly steeper under my feet. So much water was rushing up the face that it wasn't allowing me to drop down. *I'm going to get held up in the lip and go over with it*, I thought.

It eventually became so vertical that it *had* to release me and let me in. That's when I started dropping, faster and faster, until the exact point where I had seen that bump in the face in my vision; there it was. I could see my rail almost catching on it. I shifted to un-weight it for a microsecond, just enough to get over the bump. I then readjusted and regained my balance, and dropped vertically another 10 feet. As I got down to the bottom, I managed to collect myself into a stealthy low-bottom turn as I heard the thundering lip chasing me down. I could feel it right behind me, right on me. It wanted me, it wanted my bones.

I managed to crouch low and tight through the bottom turn as the white water and spray engulfed me. As I came out of the turn, wondering if I had made it or whether it was going to pick me off, I braced for impact and it catapulted and spat me out over the shoulder of the wave and into the channel. I'd done it! I'd become the first person to paddle into serious waves at Jaws!

I was stoked with adrenaline and pure joy. And a feeling of relief – it was done, it can be done, and of course I wanted more.

As I paddled back out I saw Matt get a really good one, too, but I knew if I found the right wave here, I could get barrelled – I could get properly inside the wave and ride it out. No one had ever even attempted this paddling in, but I knew this was the wave where you were more likely to get barrelled than anywhere else in the world. I knew it was all about finding the right wave. I knew they were out there. Jaws was the place for it, barrel central; you just had to be in the right place and position for take-off, to be able to backdoor them or line them up just perfectly.

I scoured the horizon for more sets. I knew what I wanted, but the wind was starting to strengthen and I was running out of time.

The next set came in and I paddled 100 metres across the line-up to see if I could get a little deeper. As the next set approached I realised I was too far across the peak, and I was very deep. I scraped over the first one and I could see that the couple behind it looked a lot bigger. I knew that if I didn't get this next one, the one behind was going to catch me and I was going to get caught inside. This one looked like I could possibly take off deep and pull into the barrel.

I didn't think about it; I didn't have time to think. I knew what I had to do; I had prepped for it in my head already, countless

times. I swivelled, turned and committed 100 per cent. I knew I had to go no matter what. I took six big, deep strokes and got to my feet, instantly angling my board across and down the face as much as possible. But as I stood up, I knew I was already way too deep. Screw it, I knew it, but I was going anyway; I wanted to get barrelled, whether I made it out or not was inconsequential in that moment.

I just wanted to pull in and watch the ocean unfold around me as I rode inside, even if only for a few split seconds. I wanted to be inside my cathedral, my church, my sanctuary, my piece of heaven – I didn't care what came after that. I just wanted to pull into that freight-train barrel at Jaws, because I knew it was possible. I was committed and locked in. That's one thing about surfing bigger waves – you have to be all in, with zero doubt, because doubt causes fear, fear causes hesitation, and hesitation will cause your worst fears to instantly become reality.

I knew I was late dropping down the face. I just tried to keep my weight on my toes and my board's nose down. I had to stay connected and push as hard as I could on that inside rail to try to pull up under the thundering lip as it came down like a guillotine next to me.

At the last second I managed to get that important edge of my board in and pull it up and quickly around as the whole barrel came down over me. But as soon as I was inside and started to draw my line and set my rail, I knew that I was far too deep and there was no way I was going to make it out of this thing. I just needed to see how far I could travel inside the barrel before it consumed me from behind and flung me forwards over the nose of my board. I rode for 20 to 30 metres and waited for what I knew was going to be a horrendous wipe-out and hold-down ...

BOOM! It sucked me back over and ripped me so violently I thought my arms were going to be pulled from my torso, as it instantly pushed me deep down into the turbulent blue spin cycle. I knew I needed to get to the surface soon to avoid the dreaded two-wave hold-down.

I was running out of air, but there was so much turbulence and aerated water that it seemed pointless to try to fight my way to the top, even though I was desperate to get a breath. I broke the surface to take a quick breath and was instantly smashed by the next wave. It threw me around like I was in a car crash, until I was deep and the turbulence eased. I managed to swim up through an air pocket to the surface. The next wave was smaller, but still rolled over me.

As I tried to pull up on my leash to get to my board on the surface, I could feel that something was wrong. My board had snapped, and there was only a three-foot tail and some ripped and stripped pieces of fibreglass at the end of the leash. I expected to see my rescue team coming to get me out – the impact zone here sort of holds you in a really bad place before letting you go. I thought as soon as I popped up they would be there, but they were nowhere to be seen. I realised right then and there that I was very much on my own.

I took two more waves on the head before escaping into the safety of the channel. Where the hell was my rescue team while I was trying to break new ground in surfing and almost dying in the process?

A few months later, I watched the video footage of that day at Jaws. It was scary and really blew me away, but I had to laugh at my so-called "safety team" on the nearby rescue ski. Although they'd said they'd be my backup, the footage showed that they were really just there to capture images and footage of the first guys to paddle into waves of consequence at Jaws, or die trying! You can hear them on the ski saying, "Oh shit, he fell." Then silence for a good couple of seconds. Then, "Maybe we should go get him?"

More silence. Then, "Why?" A painfully long silence. Then, "Because he still hasn't come up."

I laughed, but I was pretty pissed off at the time, to be honest.

Fortunately, everything worked out well and I didn't drown, but finding out that the crew I thought was my safety team was actually just a bunch of people filming me to make money off of me was a rude wake-up call. And a vital lesson. Know your team – especially your safety team. Make sure you can trust them and are confident that they've got your back. As I learnt that day, trust isn't given, it's earned!

Then again, I also firmly believe you should always be able to get yourself out of any situation you get yourself into; otherwise you shouldn't put yourself there in the first place.

An article in one of the surf magazines said I'd taken a yarn out of *In God's Hands*, a fictional movie featuring one of my big-wave heroes, Shane Dorian. In the movie, which came out the year before I made history, Shane's character paddles into Jaws. Ironically, now 15 years later, Shane is the man out at Jaws and the fearless rider everyone looks up to, including me.

But making history doesn't automatically buy you a meal ticket – or a flight home. My life has never been a smooth ride. Whenever I achieve something, fate always seems to put another obstacle in my way. This time it was my clothing sponsor.

I had no money to fly from Maui back to Hawaii in order to catch my flight home. I needed $60 for the plane ticket. So I phoned my clothing sponsor in South Africa at the time.

"Hey, guys, I've just made history here by paddling into Jaws, but I'm stuck at the airport with no money. Can you loan me $60 for the ticket?"

"Yeah, that's awesome, Chris," they said. "But what you're doing over there doesn't really have any bearing or impact on what we're doing here in South Africa, so sorry, can't help you out. But hey, good job!"

I was furious. I slammed down the phone and ripped all the sponsor's stickers off my backup board. Then I wrote "For Sale" on it and flogged it at the airport to be able to pay for a ticket back to Oahu.

The South African surf industry often seems to think that helping you represent your country involves giving you a couple of pairs of board shorts, some T-shirts and a few stickers. It's why so few of our top surfers have made it internationally. It's difficult coming from South Africa, with so little support. Standing at the airport that day, selling my only backup board in order to get home, I realised that if I wanted to make it in big-wave surfing, and in life, I could never rely on other people. I had to rely on myself and make it happen on my own.

The only person you can rely on 100 per cent in life, the only person who will never let you down, is yourself. So have more trust, faith and belief in yourself; because once you realise this, you can do anything.

6

Doldrums

Don't fence me in

It was never my intention to "make my mark" on big-wave surfing. The Big Four trip was a personal mission to surf the biggest waves I could find and get this obsession out of my system. Now that I'd done that (by swapping Teahupoo for Jaws), I assumed I could just move on with my life. But things rarely turn out exactly the way we plan.

I'd become the first South African to surf Mavericks. I'd paddled into and surfed the biggest wave in the world that year at Todos Santos, and won an award that I didn't even know existed. I'd become the first documented person in the world to paddle into serious waves at Jaws. After all the publicity and media coverage – on the internet, a double-page spread in *Surfer*, a feature in *Surfing* and the cover of *Zigzag* – I thought I'd get offered good local or international sponsorship. But it never happened. So I told myself it was time to return home, settle down, get a job and start a regular life. I figured I would get the house with the white picket fence and the Jack Russell, get married and have kids. But I was wrong.

Big waves *weren't* out of my system. As much as I tried to move on, now that I'd really had a taste of the biggest and best of them,

my desire to chase them and ride them had only strengthened. I tried to ignore the pull. For three whole years I tried to put it out of my mind, but I was just really unhappy. Every time I saw a big swell appearing on the charts somewhere in the world, I'd get anxious, irritated and depressed that I wasn't there to surf it. It must be how a drug addict feels when they aren't able to get their fix. It's like this torturous, irritating, sickening feeling that won't go away, and it just gets worse and worse as the swell approaches. And then the reports start coming in from your friends saying that the waves were epic. And that makes it even worse, hearing what you missed out on. It's horrendous.

I had taken a job as Billabong South Africa's national sales and promotional manager, based in Jeffreys Bay. For the next two years I just put my head down and worked really hard. So hard, in fact, that I hardly got in the water at all. Eventually I realised that having a great job title, a good salary and a seven-hour drive to Cape Town every alternate weekend to see family and friends wasn't really making me happy. And there was something else – I wasn't getting to do the one thing in life that *really* made me happy: surf really big waves.

I'd lost my sense of humour. When you're working so hard, you get so absorbed and caught up in it all that you don't have time to come up and take a breath. I always said to myself that if I didn't like the person I was becoming and if I lost my sense of humour in whatever I was doing, then it was time to make a change and move on. So I resigned and headed over to the UK to get some international work experience. I wanted to be based where there was more direct access to California and Hawaii, and earn pounds so that I could afford to get there.

I spent a grand total of one week in London before I needed to get out. I was landlocked in the Big Smoke and my gills were drying up. I just needed to get back to the water. On advice from

Ross, a really good Australian friend who worked with me at Billabong in J-Bay, I went to Jersey, in the Channel Islands. I put my CV out there and then couldn't understand why no one was getting back to me. I had just come from a great position at Billabong South Africa, so I'd expected to at least get a foot in the door. Then someone told me that they don't hire anybody who wasn't from Jersey for key managerial roles and I should look at getting work as a waiter or barman.

So I'd flown all the way from London to live and work in the Channel Islands as a barman. Not ideal. I heard about a stationery company that was looking for sales people. I applied and was told that I could have the job, but I would have to wear a suit and tie. Another first for me. But I wanted to grow up and get serious, do what the rest of my contemporaries were doing, and so, at the age of 28, I bought my first suit and tie. Trying to remember how to tie a Windsor knot while looking in the mirror was entertaining.

I think I was there just over three weeks before the email came from home saying it was sunny and the waves were cranking at 8 to 10 feet, and asking if I would be around in August to compete in the 2003 Red Bull Big Wave Africa event, as I had made the invite list of 24 surfers.

Let's see: I was stuck in the freezing cold, not really enjoying what I was doing, not making decent money, wearing a suit and tie, with a boss who was a complete wanker. When I let him know that I might need to take a week off in August to fly out for this super-elite, world-class event on short notice, he told me I had to make a choice. What was more important to me: my job, or surfing a big-wave event in South Africa that may or may not happen?

I could have told him that when you're a big-wave surfer at heart, you travel around the world and pretty much drop everything when the waves are 15 to 20 feet, no matter where you are

or what and how much you have to sacrifice. I could have told him that big-wave surfing is an obsession; it's hardwired into me, like a character trait. I could have told him that you don't choose it, it chooses you. But I realised that I would be wasting my breath trying to explain it to him. The fact that he could even think of asking me to choose between sliding down massive, deep, open-ocean monsters and selling ballpoint pens to other suits kind of said it all.

That was my last day in a suit and tie. I was glad to tick that box and move swiftly on!

I ended up working at the Jersey airport as a baggage handler while I waited for the Big Wave Africa event to be called. I carried on training as much as I could, running, swimming, underwater training and surfing, and met up with some locals from the Jersey Surf School, one of them a girl called Lindsey Wilson. Special people come into your life at important junctions, for good reason. These are the ones who become friends for life; you might not see them for years, but the connection stays strong and constant, no matter the time that passes. You're not able to put a price tag on good friends like these, and Lindsey's friendship right then was priceless.

I worked at the Jersey Surf School with her for a while, coaching British Surfing Association level-two instructors and doing training camps for kids. It's always great to give back, and especially to watch kids learn to surf: the big smiles that light up their faces, to see how stoked they get when they catch that first wave; it's beautiful.

As I trained obsessively for the Big Wave Africa event, I learnt an important lesson about my body. You've got to put in to get out, and not just in terms of training – I was putting in a huge amount of that. What I *wasn't* putting in was nutrition, to the point that, after three months of intense five-hours-a-day, six-days-a-week training, my progress started to go backwards. I couldn't work out what I was doing wrong. What I hadn't realised was that I was breaking down more muscle mass and tissue than I was building up, because I wasn't putting enough sustenance back into my body. I was actually getting weaker and weaker. When my training started going backwards, I realised that I needed to find a solution, so I started researching sports nutrition.

I soon realised the truth in the saying "your body is a temple" and how important it is to put the right amount of the right nutrients into your body if you want to get peak performance out of it. Proper nutrition is an essential part of training, but it's one that many athletes don't emphasise enough. You're not able to get by on burgers, beers and chips and expect your body to work at its optimum. It seems so obvious, in hindsight. When I look back, I'm amazed that I couldn't see it at the time. But sometimes you are so absorbed in what you are doing that you're not able to see the wood from the trees.

I had turned into a little scrawny prawn. My friends said I looked really skinny and unhealthy, but I thought I was a lean, mean surfing machine. Sometimes you don't see what everyone else sees. That was a great lesson: learn to listen and take critical advice from the people closest to you, the people you trust, the ones who know you better than anyone else, who understand and support you, and have your best interests at heart. If you won't listen to them, who will you listen to?

Of course, the rider to that is that you are a reflection of the company you keep, so keep good company! It will help you more than you know in times when you really need it.

I went back to South Africa for the Red Bull event and ended up doing really well. I got shacked off my pip (barrelled) in every practice session, but got knocked out in the main event in the

111

semis. I was really bummed; I was so fit, focused and committed to doing well that year. It made me realise that you really have to enjoy the journey and not just the destination, because you may not always get there. It's great to be focused and committed, but sometimes obsessive focus on something for too long can drag you down and lead you off the path. You need to be able to stop every now and again and check yourself, realign where you are now with where you are going, assess what's working and what's not, and then be prepared to make some changes to bring yourself back into balance.

Sacrifices and silver linings

Back in the UK I applied for a position as head of a clothing division for Gul International, a big wetsuit brand. They asked to see me for an interview, so I flew over from Jersey. I arrived in London and headed to the station to catch a bus down to Newquay in Cornwall, where Gul International had its head office. I arrived late in the evening, just in time to get the last bus to Newquay, which would get me there an hour before my meeting in the morning.

I was travelling light, just a small bag with clothes for the interview and two brand-new boards. As I was loading my boards onto the bus, the driver stopped me and said, "Sorry, mate, no surfboards on the bus."

"You must be joking. I'm going down to Newquay and taking these boards with me." I pointed out that there was nothing on their website about boards not being allowed on the bus, and even offered to pay extra to have them on. But he was adamant.

"Legally, I'm not allowed to take those surfboards on the bus. If I let you load them and somebody finds out, I could lose my job. Sorry."

My first look at Mavericks, 2001: exciting, daunting …

Pure joy – cutback at Mavericks, 2001

With Jeff Clark, my friend and inspiration, at Mavericks, 2001

One of my favourite barrels ever at Dungeons, 2003

Surfing the Cribbar in Cornwall in 2006, just before pulling into a giant barrel

An amazing view of getting barrelled at Dunes in Kommetjie, 2007

Dropping into a beast at Dungeons – one of the biggest waves ridden in South Africa in 2007

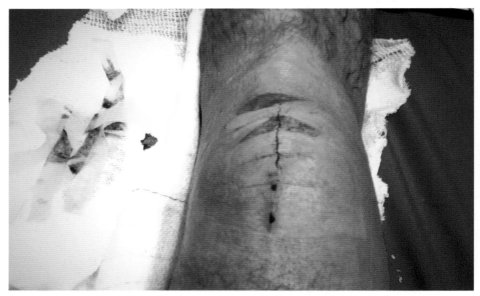

Following my accident in Chile, this is what my knee looked like just after surgery, 2008

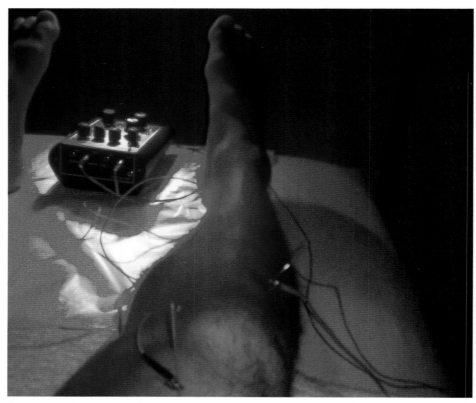

Acupuncture on my knee and rehab – and I hate needles

My favourite pic bottom-turning at Mavericks. This was the session with the broken ribs, after which I finally got an invite to the event

Mavericks: At peace … waiting … watching … content …

Ryan Seelbach and I on one of the biggest waves of the 2009 Mavericks season

I managed to find this big one in the final of the 2009 Nelscott Paddle-In Classic International

Celebrations after a great result: third place in the 2009 Nelscott Paddle-In Classic International

One of my worst moments, getting caught inside at Mavericks ... not for the faint-hearted

The semi-final of the 2010 Mavericks Invitational: going down into my low-speed bottom turn

The first wave of the final. I had to make a very important decision – one that would change the outcome of my life

On Jeff Clark's jet ski during the event – the best guy to have on your team

Surfing the biggest wave in the semi-finals with Carlos Burle, one of my heroes and a true legend

The final wave in the final of the 2010 Mavericks Invitational. Even after this wave and the event was finished, I had no idea that I had won

Enjoying every part of this life-changing moment, holding my $50 000 cheque

The bus was leaving in the next three minutes. I stood on the platform in agony.

At critical points in our lives we often get presented with hard choices. It's as if life puts you at a crossroads to test how badly you want something. These junctions are usually more important than we can see at the time. And they often require sacrifice.

What was the right choice? If I missed the bus I was going to miss the interview. It was a really important opportunity, with a good company. As much as I enjoyed being a surf instructor, I wanted to get back into business. But I was being asked to sacrifice my boards!

It was one of the hardest decisions. I took my two brand-new boards from under my arm, set them down on the platform, turned my back on them and got on the bus. They sat there alone, abandoned, as the door closed behind me and the bus reversed out of the station. I never saw those boards again.

The silver lining was that the interview went really well and I got the job. It was a pleasure to work for Gul International. I worked with a great crew of people and reported to Gul's national sales director, Mike Pickering, with whom I got on really well. Over the next three years I helped launch Gul clothing into 150 stores around the UK and the Channel Islands. I also joined the Gul International sailing team, sailing all over the UK, and surfed for the Gul surf team. It was awesome, probably the best job I have ever had.

During that time I became part of the UK surf scene, largely thanks to a spot called the Cribbar, which breaks off the end of the Towan Headland in Newquay.

The Cribbar apparently had been discovered by a couple of Aussie lifeguards in the early seventies, but they had only surfed it a few times and when it was small, in the eight-foot range. It only

broke in very specific conditions, but I took one look at the spot set-up and knew that it held the potential to be something special and deliver proper waves of magnitude and consequence. I wanted to make sure that when it did, I would be there to capitalise.

The headland had a great view of the wave, and each day for over six months I sat up there with a bag of pistachio nuts, eating them and patiently watching the wave, working it out, noting every time it broke, and recording the exact conditions it worked on and when. I'd look at the weather forecast, at the swell size, the wind direction, what the tide was doing – all the factors that make a world of difference to a specific location. I printed out forecasts and analysed the effects of the prevailing conditions and weather systems. I worked out everything, including all the hazards and the safe zones.

I knew that when the conditions were exactly right, my window of opportunity would most likely be only two to three hours, and I needed to be prepared and ready. I worked out my exit and entry points and spent a lot of time in the pool, training and fine-tuning my underwater regime, keeping fit and focused on the goal.

I'd been in Newquay for about eight months when the weather chart turned into my happy colours: a huge storm was forecast to hit the UK. Two days before the storm arrived I knew the conditions were going to be perfect.

I phoned Mike. I could have asked him for time off to surf any time – he was that kind of boss – but I never had. This time I was making an exception, because I knew the Cribbar was going to be on and it looked like I was going to have a maximum window of about three hours. He was wholeheartedly supportive and everything went according to plan. There was 15 to 18 feet of solid, clean groundswell. I paddled out in pristine, perfect conditions, and within 10 minutes of getting out to the backline the first big set came in and started standing up, and I knew I was in the perfect spot for it. I paddled hard, got to my feet, dropped in and saw immediately that I could possibly get barrelled, so I quickly changed my line and drew up and pulled into this massive barrel going right.

I didn't make it out, but I was blown away by how big and perfect it was, not to mention the fact that I had just got this giant barrel on my first wave out there. I collected myself and paddled back out, still sort of in shock. By the time I got to the back, the next set looked like it was already starting to build. I managed to paddle over the first and looked perfectly set up for the second, but I took one look at the left and knew I had to go. I took off late, managed to drop down and push hard off the bottom, and then up into another big barrel going left! This was the first time this had ever happened to me; to this day I've never experienced that anywhere else in the world, not at that size.

I surfed by myself for about three hours. I was getting a lot of great waves and a couple of big barrels on the right. It was simply incredible! On my fourth or fifth wave I got hammered by a really big 18-footer. When I surfaced I looked up at the cliffs and saw over 300 people lined up on the headland. I turned to look behind me to see what was going on – I thought maybe a boat had capsized or somebody was being rescued. But then I realised they were all lined up to watch me surf, as no one had ever ridden the Cribbar at that size!

I carried on surfing, getting unbelievable waves, until some muppet on a mini-mal, with no idea, paddled out. Without trying to sound cool, I tried to warn him that the waves were a lot bigger than he thought and that he needed to be careful. I suggested he sit on the side and just watch for a while.

As I was busy warning him, a big set came in and we both got caught inside. His board almost speared me in the head when he just bailed right in front of me. His leash instantly snapped, as he

didn't have the right equipment, and he started freaking out. After getting him through the set, I had to give him my board to paddle on, while I swam him all the way around the headland – about a two-kilometre swim – to get him to a safe area. The rescue services came and took him off my hands as we got around to the calm side. After they'd dropped him off I hitched a lift back to the point with them and caught a couple more waves.

It turned out to be a big day in British big-wave surfing history. I was on the front page of the *Newquay Voice* and featured on page three of *The Sun*, one of Britain's biggest tabloids, right next to some really nice big-breasted women. It was even on CNN and the national BBC news.

It was the perfect warm-up for the following year's Big Wave Africa.

Dungeons roars

When it's summer in the UK, it's winter down south in my home-town of Cape Town, which means the serious swells pull in and Africa's premier big wave starts lighting up.

Since I first started surfing Dungeons, it has attained inter-national status, in large part thanks to Greg Long – now one of the most famous big-wave riders in the world and a phenomenal athlete – who first came to South Africa in 2001 to take part in the Red Bull Big Wave Africa invitational. I had met him the previous year at Todos Santos, during my Big Four trip. The Red Bull event not only brought Greg and other top international stars like Carlos Burle and Jamie Sterling out to South Africa, but really helped put Dungeons on the international map. Every year I made sure I was fit and available for the competition, whether it ran or not, not only because it was a way to connect with my home base, but also because it kept my eye on another prize: the Mavericks

Invitational, the most prestigious big-wave surfing competition of them all.

With all these big-wave events, you not only have to be in it to win it, you also have to be seen to be committed to surfing the waves regularly and consistently make a positive impression out there at these spots. You have to stand out by constantly pushing the limits in order to get invited in the first place. Only 24 people in the world are invited each year to each of these events. It means having to be available to spend months at a time travelling around the world and waiting for the right conditions. As much as I loved working with the folks at Gul, who were always super supportive of my need to surf, I knew I couldn't ask for that much time off.

So in 2006 I resigned and made some travel plans. Lindsey was getting married in Fiji, and my girlfriend Tashi Dowse and I had been saving up to attend the wedding. I wanted to fulfil a long-time dream of mine and visit Rapa Nui (Easter Island) while we were over on that side of the world.

That was one thing about working in the UK; it gave me the opportunity to travel to places I would never have got to living and working in South Africa and earning South African rands. I wanted to try to get to one other big-wave spot while I had the time and a little money: Arica in Chile.

My travels started well – I flew home to South Africa after training in the UK the whole of the summer and finished third in the 2006 Red Bull Big Wave Africa. I had wanted to do well in that event, against the world's best, for as long as I could remember, so I was pretty stoked. When I got back to the UK, Tash had hung a huge congratulations sign from the balcony of our apartment, which made me feel very proud. More than anyone else, she had seen all the hard work, training, sacrifice and dedication that had gone into making it happen.

It was a great start to my travels. But, by the end, my hopes

and chances of getting that dream invite into the Mavericks Invitational would be seriously threatened unless I could get back over to California at the end of the year. So I made that my plan. Travel to the wedding, visit Easter Island and Chile, and then go back to the UK to save up enough money before heading back to California for two months over their winter. I knew it's what I had to do, no matter what, if I was to finally realise that lifelong goal and dream.

Islands

The wedding in Fiji was magical. It was on a rustic little island, right on the outskirts of the Fijian island chain. It was just a super special time in a beautiful place with beautiful people and close friends. We spent lots of evenings dancing and drinking Cava, and there were a couple of good waves on the island, too.

After the wedding, Tash and I flew out to the most remote island on the planet: Rapa Nui. The nearest populated landmass is 2 075 kilometres away. And the nearest continental point is Chile, at 3 512 kilometres away. Most people know it as Easter Island, home of the famous monolithic human faces, called *moai*, which the islanders carved to appease their gods. They became so consumed with creating and transporting these statues that they completely deforested their island. I went to a few of the quarries, and it was eerie; you can make out faces and bodies half-carved out of rock, forever incomplete.

We hired a small 4 x 4, packed our camping gear and set out to explore the island, which is only 30 kilometres long and five kilometres wide. I ended up surfing a few really fun and unique locations solo. There were a few reef breaks about a kilometre offshore that produced some heavy waves. Being so isolated and unable to rely on anybody if you get injured brings a certain purity to surfing.

But the biggest thing I took away from my time on Rapa Nui had nothing to do with the size or quality of the waves. It really felt like the island took me to the core of my sport and what it was all about. The simple things in life that make us happy.

The Rapa Nui people are incredible watermen. The islanders are renowned for holding a tribal island race in which the top athletes and warriors of each tribe compete. It's called the Birdman Race, and it gives new meaning to the term "extreme sports". It's the most insane race I've ever seen: the route includes climbing down a 300-metre-high vertical cliff, then diving into the sea from 20 metres up and swimming for over a kilometre across a shark-infested stretch of water to Bird Island. Once there, the athletes have to steal an egg from the nest of an indigenous bird, carry it back across the shark-infested water, climb back up the steep cliff with no rope, and run up the almost-sheer vertical terrain back to the start. The first one back with their egg intact is the winner and leads the tribes on the island for the following five years. It's about a 30-kilometre round trip, and all the while you're competing against warriors from other tribes who are doing everything from trying to squash your egg to actually killing you.

Rapa Nui made me rethink a lot of things in my life. The more stuff we accumulate, the more bills and the more problems we seem to have. The more we have in this world, the more we betray the human race, our soul, our spirit and our inner child. The more clutter we have – from cellphones and computers to Facebook and Twitter – the more complicated and hectic life gets, and the less time we have to stop and appreciate the simple things, to live and be in the moment.

On Rapa Nui we slept under the stars, and I have never to this day seen such a beautiful night sky – when the lights go out in the island's main village at 11 p.m., the closest light interference is literally thousands of miles away.

Simplicity is wisdom. Life should be about simplifying everything, breaking it down and keeping it as basic as possible. The best things and the small things in life are still free, and those are the ones we often take for granted: friends, family, the ocean, nature and the ability to appreciate everything around us. That's what Rapa Nui taught me never to forget.

Chile

My next trip was plagued with troubles from the start. I just seemed to hit stumbling block after stumbling block. Sometimes when this happens, you have to ask yourself if there's a reason why these obstacles keep coming up, and whether perhaps you shouldn't be doing what you're doing. It's hard to stop and listen to this intuitive voice – especially when you are as stubborn and focused on a goal as I tend to be!

When I got word that a big swell was heading for Chile, I booked my ticket. I was super excited to test some of the legendary South Pacific big waves. I packed a couple of boards, a tow board and a big-wave paddle-in gun, and headed off.

That's when I discovered that international terrorist threats can affect even the most Zen surfer. The 2006 transatlantic aircraft plot to bomb seven planes paralysed Heathrow for a day. My flight was cancelled and I was stranded, along with 40 000 other travellers. Four days later, when I finally touched down in Santiago, the big swell had been and gone and I had missed it.

I wasn't going to let that stop me, though, so I hooked a connecting flight up to the northern tip of Chile and Iquique, home of the infamous Chilean big barrels I'd been researching for years.

Northern Chile is arid. When I arrived, I asked the taxi driver in broken Spanish how often it rained. He told me it didn't really rain. "You mean like only once a month?" His reply made me realise the severity of the water shortage: "No, I think it rained about six years ago!"

Overlooking the coast are huge red mountains that loom over 1 500 metres high. They look like something out of *Star Wars*. It's quite surreal being in the water and looking back at this amazing, hazy landscape.

I stayed at the Iquique Backpackers' Hostel, a great little place just in front of the beach and run by a wonderful South American girl called Daniela. I hooked up with Tyler Bruer, an old surf buddy from the United States. Good friends are hard to find, but when the shit hits the fan, you're not able to put a price tag on good mates, as I would be reminded in the days to come.

The Iquique waves were small. I went down to the beach on the second day and saw some guys playing around in the shore break, in literally two-foot waves, towing in behind a ski. I thought, why not? I ran back to my hostel, grabbed my tow board and asked a guy in Spanish if I could get a couple of goes. I'd been doing a lot of tow-in surfing in the UK, trying loops and rodeo flips and stuff, so I was pretty keen to get wet and have a couple of rides while the waves were small.

He agreed to tow me into the little beachy shore break, and I started practising some new-age, small-wave aerial manoeuvres and flips. On my fifth wave I did a big aerial manoeuvre and, as I came down, my front foot slipped out of the foot strap and my knee went straight into the stringer of the board. I remember thinking to myself, *That doesn't feel good. Whatever I just did, I caused some serious damage.*

When I got up, I couldn't stand on my leg properly; it was sort of floating to the inside. I put my hand down onto my kneecap and only felt half of it. I didn't know it yet, but I had basically shattered my kneecap into about eight pieces. What I did know was that I'd done something pretty bad in a very remote village in the most northern part of Chile.

A couple of people on the beach came to help me. They put me in a makeshift sling and took me back to the hostel. And then Tyler and Daniela took over – I really don't know what I would have done without those two, they were amazing. They got me to the hospital and the doctor took one look at me and said, "You need to go in for surgery now; you've broken your kneecap. We need to pin all the pieces back together." Of course this was all in Spanish and I couldn't understand half the stuff he was saying. But there was no way I was getting operated on right then and there.

The doc stared at me with these heavily bloodshot eyes and then started shouting at me in Spanish. I think he was pretty pissed off with the fact that I wanted to get surgery done in a "proper" hospital, with a surgeon that didn't look and act like he was completely stoned, in a place where I could understand what they were telling me. So he took a scalpel and sliced the side of my knee open, let all the goo and fluid run out, put a little plaster over it and said, "Okay, you can go now."

"What about antibiotics or anti-inflammatories or crutches?" I asked him. A decent painkiller would have been nice, too.

"You don't want to be operated on," he said, "so there's nothing else I can do for you. *Adios las vamos*, see you later, cheers."

Daniela and Tyler drove me around to find a pair of second-hand crutches. In the days to follow I would also be super grateful to my good friend Sarah in the UK who had forced me to sort out my travel insurance before I left. It turned out to be some of the best advice ever, as without it I would have been screwed.

It took me three days to get an emergency flight back to the UK – it was a local holiday and all the flights were full. When a seat finally became available I had to pretend there was nothing wrong with my leg – the airline's rules said that to travel with a broken leg you required two seats, and there weren't two seats available. Having to walk onto the plane with my backpack as if there was nothing wrong with my leg took me to a whole other level of mind power and determination. I needed to get to the UK for surgery, but there were risks to flying with a broken leg. By the time I arrived at Heathrow after flying 32 hours with no real painkillers, I was in agony and my leg had swollen to twice its normal size.

A nurse met me at the gate with a wheelchair, and wheeled me straight through customs and into the back of an ambulance. We drove directly to the hospital in Truro, where there was a surgeon waiting to operate on my knee that same night.

After the operation I lay in the hospital bed thinking about how I'd wasted half the Chile trip. Besides being a place I'd always wanted to go, that trip was supposed to be my preparation for California at the end of the year. I was scheduled to leave in two and a half months' time, to coincide with the beginning of the Mavericks season in November. But the surgeon had other ideas.

"My friend, you won't be surfing any time soon. You're looking at six months to a year's recovery time, and a minimum of six months before you can even think of getting back in the water."

As grateful as I was for the top-notch medical facilities that could sort out my knee, I told him I was going to California and Hawaii in two months' time.

"It's literally impossible," he said. "You only come out of the cast in six weeks' time, which means you want to leave two weeks after that? There's no chance – you'll see what I mean when you come out of that cast."

So I made a deal with him. I told him I would move my trip out by two weeks and meet with him in 10 weeks' time to make a decision then. I knew he was just humouring me when he shook his head, smiled and agreed. "Okay then," I told him. "We're on."

That's when my recovery started.

Mind power

It's amazing what you can achieve when you have a lifelong goal in sight, when you believe in it strongly enough and will do anything to get there.

After three screws, a whole lot of wire, six weeks in a cast and an 8- to 12-month full-recovery prognosis, rumours started circulating that I would never be able to surf again. Yeah right ... not if I could help it!

I'd been planning my winter surf trip to Northern California and Hawaii for years. I wasn't going to let a busted knee get in my way.

I followed the recommended post-operative therapy, and then some. I took every kind of bone and cartilage supporting and healing tablet you can imagine – calcium, glucosamine and chondroitin – I even started drinking milk, and I'm lactose intolerant! I had acupuncture every day, which will amaze anyone who knows about my phobia of needles.

One week after coming out of the cast, I was teaching a jet-ski rescue course – definitely not doctor's orders, but I believe we need to push our bodies to heal. A week after that, I went surfing for the first time. I couldn't straighten my knee properly, but enough to stand up, even though it was really uncomfortable and very difficult to bend with the two braces I had on. It was like learning to surf all over again.

Every night as I lay in bed, I visualised my knee healing. I pictured the blood flowing, bringing recuperative oxygen and minerals; I visualised the bones knitting and the cartilage growing, the ligaments and tendons pulling it all together ...

Two weeks before I flew out to California, I met with the surgeon again. He was both shocked and amazed at the progress I had made, but he still couldn't get his head around the idea of me surfing.

"I don't really know how you got to this point so quickly – it is simply astonishing," he said. "I've never seen anyone heal that quickly. But if you fall in big surf, with your leg being so fragile, you could do some serious damage – so much so that you might not be able to walk properly in the future."

It only took me a split second to come back with the answer: "Well, then I won't fall!"

Looking back on that moment, I realise it's probably one of the cockiest things I've ever said. But the crazy thing is, I wasn't trying to be a smartass. I said it without even thinking. I just believed it to be true, with 100 per cent conviction, with every fibre of my being.

Two weeks later I flew out to California, and 10 days after that Jeff Clark invited me to be his tow partner in the Nelscott Reef Big Wave event. It was a dream come true, one that could bring me a step closer to a Mavericks invitation. I competed in the event with one knee brace under my wetsuit, two over it, and the whole thing wrapped in duct tape. The surf was pumping 40-foot, flawless, clean waves. We competed against the world's best and finished fifth overall. And, amazingly enough, for the first time in my over 20 years of big-wave surfing, on that magical day of competing in massive surf, I never fell once!

That's why I know what I'm talking about when I tell people that if you truly believe in yourself and what's possible, and if you use the power of your mind to visualise, you will be amazed by what you can achieve. What you believe, you achieve, and what you don't, you won't.

Mavericks had been dogging me for the better part of a decade – since the millennium, in fact. No matter where I went and what I did, my dream to be one of the titans of Mavericks, to compete in the Mavericks Invitational, the most prestigious big-wave surfing

competition in the world, was right there with me. But it was the one goal that also kept eluding me.

As the name suggests, you have to be invited to compete in it. The selection panel is hardcore and it's the toughest invite list to crack in big-wave surfing. They keep an eye on those who are not only consistently surfing Mavericks but, more specifically, those who charge it harder than anyone else and are constantly pushing the boundaries out in the water. They are looking for the standouts at the spot each season, the surfers who show a real commitment to Mavericks, go for the biggest and meanest waves that exist and consistently make them – preferably in mind-blowing style.

Basically, they want to see you coming back year after year and excelling time and again before they will give you an invite to the event. It doesn't matter if you come from Cape Town or Half Moon Bay in California; it's about consistently giving high-end performances in massive surf at Mavericks.

As I've said before, only 24 people in the world are invited to the event each year. These are literally the best big-wave riders on the planet. There is also an alternate invite list of another 10 names. The alternates are the surfers who almost made the main list. They are the ones who will be called on if any of the other 24 surfers are not able to make it due to injury when the event takes place. I had been on and off that alternate list for almost nine years now, and as much as it was a huge honour and recognition to be on it, I just wanted to make the main event – I wanted to be one of the first 24. I wanted to be one of the Mavericks Titans, one of the 24 elite invitees.

Since 2000, I had tried to go over as often as I could. But, as I was not a professional paid athlete, it was tough finding the money and balancing work demands and paying the bills, even more so when I returned to South Africa.

It was now 2008, the year I had decided would be my last

opportunity and the last time I would attempt to get an invite to the prestigious Mavericks Invitational, as I had now given up almost 10 years for this and I needed to realise when to say "enough is enough" – I had already sacrificed so much. I had been back in South Africa for three years, running O'Neill South Africa, and had decided to start my own small company the following year. So I planned a well-deserved break when I finished up in order to focus on reaching for that elusive Mavericks invite and to give me more flexibility to be able to take time off to chase that dream, no matter what.

In November 2008, before flying out, I knew that this was the last year I was going to be able to chase my dream to get that elusive invite, as I had now given up almost 10 years for this one goal. I needed to realise when to say enough is enough, as I had already sacrificed so much.

The Mavericks Big Wave Invitational is not like any other competition, as it happens over a five-month waiting period and can be called at any time within that time span, with only 48 hours' notice. It happens between November and March (the northern-hemisphere winter), when the conditions look like they are going to be perfect. All participants are then given two days to get there before the event starts. If the conditions don't occur and aren't conducive for the event to run (clean 40-foot-plus faces for eight hours during daylight hours, with no wind or very light offshore winds), then the event doesn't run at all that year!

I could only afford to go over for four weeks in 2008/09, after finishing up for O'Neill in late November, and unfortunately for me, the only big swell that came in that season happened two weeks before I was able to fly out and so I missed it. It was soul-destroying seeing it form and head for California while I was back in South Africa, not able to get there to charge it with all the other big-wave riders and make my mark.

To add insult to injury, the day before I was due to fly out, I competed in a stand-up paddleboarding (SUP) wave contest, which I shouldn't have done. I knew it at the time, but I did it anyway and I paid the price. To my absolute horror, I came down from a manoeuvre in the semi-finals and tore the media cartilage ligament in my right knee. I felt it pull and stretch and tear, and then my whole body started shaking and trembling. I knew I had done something really bad. I went straight to the top physiotherapist to try to find out just *how* bad. The doctor said I had a level-two, borderline level-three tear, which meant I could either go for surgery or wait and try to rehabilitate it and see how that went. He recommended six to eight weeks of rehab before I would be able to surf properly again. Thanks, universe, for yet another obstacle!

Distraught, I postponed my flight by a week. I went to a specialist physio, who gave me a good brace and repeated the doctor's advice that I needed to take it easy for the next six to eight weeks. I knew I needed to take more drastic action.

Anybody who knows me will tell you that there is only one thing in life I'm scared of, and that's needles. But in the next few days I went to the top acupuncturist in South Africa and asked him to stick me full of needles. He stuck needles in my head and he stuck needles in my knee. I asked him: "Is there anything I'm going to get freaked out by?"

"Just as long as you don't look, you'll be fine."

After 20 minutes of him putting in various types of needles, I opened my eyes. There was one long needle sticking out of the side of my knee. I asked him about it.

"That," he said, "is one of the longer needles that goes right through your knee from one side to the other."

I almost passed out right then and there. But I went back to him twice more before I flew out.

In California I phoned Hiday, a really good friend who is also a pretty special acupuncturist. In fact, he comes from a long line of Chinese acupuncturists, going back 3 000 years. I managed to get him to see me twice a week for a month to get my knee right before the first swells started hitting. I also went down to Santa Cruz and spent a lot of time just pool-training, since that was all I could do to keep fit and rehab my knee, as surfing wasn't an option.

My knee was feeling a whole lot better after a couple of weeks. So while I waited for the swells to kick in, I added a lot of under-water training and some light paddleboarding – mostly flat-water paddling and small, tiny SUP surfs – to my training regime. Most people don't understand how frustrating it is when you've been training twice a day, six days a week, for over 120 days, and you've got up to peak fitness and then suddenly you're not able to train properly, and you're sitting in California, spending a lot of money to be there, in the freezing cold in the middle of winter, not drink-ing, not going out and, on top of all that, not being able to surf! It's probably the most frustrating, depressing thing on the planet.

As it happened, 2008/09 was the worst season that I can remember since I started going over to Mavericks. As I said, the only big swell was that one at the beginning of November – which I missed. Other than that, there were a couple of 10- and 15-foot swells, but that was it for the whole season. None of the swells came even close to the calibre required to even call the Mavericks Invitational.

Jeff Clark and I ended up tow-surfing Mavericks by ourselves on Christmas Day in Santa hats – it was the first surf I'd had since injuring myself the month before, but a Christmas surf with my good friend Jeff couldn't have been a better end to a challenging year. I waited until the middle of January and even went to the event's opening ceremony, seeing as I was there and

was so keen to get that one chance, that one opportunity, to get that invite for the following season's event to compete against the world's best, in the biggest and heaviest paddle-in waves on the planet.

I was so close, yet so far. I had been working towards this goal for so long. I just wanted to know if I was really as good as the best, so I could be happy, content, tick the box and move on with my life. I'd told myself that this was going to be the last season of trying, no matter what, because when I got back home this time around, I would need to devote all my time, money and energy to my new company. There was a good chance that after this trip, if I didn't crack an invite, I might never come back.

My time in California was quickly running out, and with it my finances and the chance of having a go at the Mavericks Invitational. The sea gods, it seemed, just weren't in the mood. But I couldn't accept that after all this time and effort, after almost 10 years of trying, Mavericks wasn't to be.

For the first time ever I started to wonder whether I was wasting my time, money and energy on a goal that just seemed to be doing everything in its power to elude and evade me. Maybe I needed to think of moving on. In low times you often question yourself and your beliefs, and this is when you really need to remain strong and focused on your goal – to never give up and never give in.

And then it happened: a beautiful purple blob appeared in the middle of the weather chart.

I'd been watching the charts obsessively as the day of my departure approached. I was into the last five days before I had to fly home and now, finally, there it was!

The swell was forecast to arrive two days before I had to fly out. And it was a big one. This was going to be my last chance to make an impression. So two days before it arrived I headed out to one of the beach breaks for a small surf to catch some warm-up waves.

I was amped!

Then, halfway through the surf, while we were just messing around, I got T-boned in my ribs by my own board. I felt two of my ribs give way. I was winded, sore and broken. I lay in the water groaning and clutching my chest as I slowly floated in next to my board. I knew I had done something bad, but I was too scared to think about what it was and how it was about to affect the next two days.

Anyone who has had cracked ribs can tell you that it is one of the most painful things you can imagine. There is absolutely nothing you can do, except let them heal. To even think of lying on a surfboard in that condition was excruciating.

But what choice did I have? This was it – if I didn't get into Mavericks this year, it was never going to happen. I had missed the first main swell of the season, so I absolutely had to surf this one, otherwise everything I had done up to this point would have been for nothing. I was not going to let that happen. In two days I would be flying home. If I didn't give it my best shot now, I knew I would always look back and wonder whether I could have done it if only I'd tried. This time it wasn't about logic or what I wanted to do; it wasn't a choice. I just knew: I *had* to do it.

Now my greatest fear was falling on a big wave. I realised that with the pain in my ribs being so excruciating, I might not be able to stop myself gasping as I hit the water – not a good thing to be concerned about when you are trying to hold your breath for what might be an extended length of time underwater.

So I went out and bought every painkiller possible. I dosed myself with Ibuprofen, anti-inflammatories, Arnica tablets, herbal concoctions and Chinese remedies. I swallowed pills and rubbed on ointments. When my fingers started to tingle and I saw purple

dots, I knew that was enough. Then I thought about how I could pad my ribs to stop them from sticking out, so I wrapped several layers of plastic cling wrap around my torso. Then I pulled on my wetsuit, sucked up the pain, took a deep breath, focused on the objective and paddled out into the biggest surf of the season.

I caught two of the biggest waves that day. Some days you just have to have the determination to dig deep and push your boundaries, let go of limiting beliefs and go beyond what most people think is possible. We all have the ability to do that, to let go of the fear, to face it, move through it and still move forwards. The key is that you have to believe you can before you can make it happen.

I always like to say there is no such thing as failure in life, only a failure to try! I also believe that you've got to be in it to win it – and thanks to that last-minute swell and my decision to try, no matter the outcome, I was in it.

A month later I finally got the news … I had done it! Thanks to that key session, surfing with two cracked ribs, I was awarded one of the 24 main slots to compete in my dream event, the infamous Mavericks Big Wave Invitational. Finally, I would be one of the Titans of Mavericks for the 2009/10 season. Epic! I was one step closer to my dream coming true.

7

Chasing Mavericks

Getting the invite to compete at Mavericks was one thing; getting there for the event itself once they called it was something else. I knew it wasn't going to be easy, but I had no idea that this was just the beginning of the universe's plan to test me to my limit, and then beyond. By the end of it all I felt like a one-man version of that TV reality show, *The Amazing Race*, where they throw all kinds of obstacles at the contestants and then watch to see whether they can actually make it to the destination. Like them, I just had to keep my eye on the prize.

I was pretty broke after funding the start-up of my sporting-brand agency. Even after being invited to compete in the world's premier big-wave event, I still couldn't get enough sponsorship together, so as always I would have to rely on my own ingenuity and finances to make it happen.

In life you can sit around and play the victim, stamp your feet and complain, or you can get up and do something about it – make a plan and make it happen.

I didn't have enough money to spend the entire winter over in the US, but I thought I could raise enough funds to stay there for two of the three months the event was most likely to run. I phoned up my close friend and former schoolmate Greg Casey, who owned

a great little pub/restaurant in Cape Town called Banana Jam, and asked him if he would lend me his restaurant so that I could host a fundraiser there that would allow me to fly over and represent South Africa in the Mavericks event. He didn't even blink. "Sure thing, Chris, I'm in!"

I spent weeks getting everything together: organising items to auction, hiring an auctioneer, signing posters and surfboards, arranging accommodation, and so on. I planned to put stickers with the names of everyone who contributed between R200 and R500 on the nose of my board so that they could come along on my journey, since they were helping me achieve my goals and dreams.

The night came and the support was overwhelming. It's amazing what kind of response you get when you ask for assistance, and how many people are willing to assist you when you genuinely need help. I raised about R30 000, which was enough to pay for my ticket and to help me stay over in California for almost three months, until the end of January 2010. I was also able to pay my assistant to look after the business while I was away.

I flew out a couple of days later full of optimism and pride. I was armed with two boards with the names of my "sponsors" all the way down the sides of the rails. The support I got from every-one strengthened my sense of self-belief, and my desire to make my hometown and country proud. I was ready to do battle, ready to do whatever it took to achieve my goal, to live my dream, and bring home the Mavericks Big Wave Invitational title and trophy. I truly believed I could do it, whether I said it to anyone or not. I knew that if I got just one chance to prove that I was as good as the best, I could show the world that you can achieve anything if you have courage, determination and the heart to believe in yourself and follow your dreams.

Of course, I had also put in four full months of relentless training; pool- and underwater-training, everyday, twice a day, before and after work, six days a week, over and above surfing. There could be no room for excuses or regrets. I was 100 per cent ready, both physically and mentally.

The season started slow, but three weeks after I arrived in California, the biggest storm of the winter popped up on the charts. It looked really promising, but as fate would have it the storm was too direct and was going to hit the Bay area straight on, making Mavericks too wild and stormy for the organisers to call the event.

But 1 000 kilometres north, in Northern Oregon, another big-wave event, the Nelscott Reef Big Wave Paddle In Classic, was raring to go. Up there they were rubbing their hands with glee, as the conditions in their neck of the woods looked to be epic, promising massive, clean waves for the event. The day before the storm hit, when they realised there was no way Mavericks was going to run, they called a green light on Nelscott.

Nelscott is also invitation-only, but as I was invited for Mavericks, and based on my results from previous years, I was automatically an invitee for Nelscott. Jeff Clark and I packed up our stuff, got in the car and headed up Highway 5 to Oregon, armed with our big-wave guns, Starbucks coffee and the ski trailing behind.

Nelscott

The weather was ferocious all the way up the coast. Wind, rain, sleet, snow, we had it all. We hoped that everything would settle in Oregon overnight and that in the morning we'd be blessed with perfect conditions. Nevertheless, we all knew that the dreaded Nelscott Reef beach break was going to be very scary and difficult to get through to get out to the wave itself, which was over two kilometres out to sea.

We managed to get some rest after being on the road all day and prepped our equipment in the evening, so we were ready for whatever the morning would bring.

As daylight broke, we could see the lines coming in; they were really big. We got all our gear together and I checked in for my heat before we headed down to the ramp from where we would launch the ski.

It took us 20 minutes and three attempts just to get through the deadly 15-foot-face shore break that was thundering in. It was heaving. Skis got flipped and people were lost overboard. It was chaos and more than a little scary. But we knew that once we were out through that shore break, we were home free. On our third attempt, just after we'd punched through an eight-foot wall of white water, we saw a gap. Jeff floored it, but at the last second we saw the next one looming up, just about to break. Jeff throttled down and we surged over the top.

We paused there for a second, with me on the back of the rescue sled, looking down as the wave ledged out below me. I was literally hanging off the edge, dangling over the draining lip, when Jeff added a burst of throttle and dropped us over the back of the wave into the clear. Shoo, we had made it! We drove the ski another kilometre out to the back line. I pulled on my vest and was good to go.

The day was amazing and really went my way. My positioning and timing were right for each set that came through. The waves were big, smooth and clean, and seemed to just come to me; before I knew it, I was in the final and feeling strong.

Entering the final I knew I had a good chance of doing well, but, like in all the big-wave events, you just never know what you're going to get. Your world can change in an instant, and it often does.

I had a great start to the heat in the final, taking off later and deeper than anyone in the water, or so I thought. When I came in everyone told me I had won, but somehow it was not to be and I ended up coming third. Some people wanted to contest the decision, but I wanted to be bigger than that. I was disappointed, but you have to learn to take your losses humbly. I knew that someday it would all come back to me. Just not this day.

It was yet another reminder that when you lose, don't lose the lesson! The lesson for me that day was that, as the lone South African, I had to make sure that I not only came out on top, but won so convincingly that no one could possibly question the result. I made that my goal for the Mavericks event.

Strategic surfing

I was given some great advice at the Nelscott event. It came from big-wave veteran and contest director Gary Linden.

Everyone thought I should have won, based on my performance. People who watched me surf said I did really well, but somehow I wasn't getting the results. I was the guy that would surf a three- or four-hour session and get phenomenal waves and then get hammered. After the event, Gary told me: "Chris, it's a numbers game."

When it comes to surfing competitions, time is everything. You have a 40-minute window in a contest heat, during which you generally need to get at least two good waves to progress to the next round. I had a tendency to go big from the get-go, which meant I often wiped out trying to go too late or deep and then had to spend time retrieving my boards.

"You're a phenomenal surfer," Gary said, "but what you need is a simple strategy."

When you only have 40-odd minutes, he told me, don't waste your heat trying to be a hero and take off under the lip and get hammered and spend half your heat swimming. The guy who is

taking off, making it and playing it fairly safe and solid is the one who'll get through his heat. Remember, you just need two average rides, as the top three in each heat advance.

"You always go for the best and the biggest waves right off and blow your chances," he said. "You need to strategise, tone yourself down a bit. Tame your beast – put it in the box!"

Basically, Gary's advice was to play it safe until I had two solid waves under my belt, and then let rip.

"Once you've ticked off the two you need to get through the heat, you can release your beast and go crazy!"

He was right. I had a tendency to go gung-ho on the first wave I could. But in big-wave surfing, the sets can come 10 to 15 minutes apart, which means you might only get two or three sets in a heat. You have to make every wave count.

The playing field is massive, and to be in the right place is also difficult. And when you're surfing at this level, against the best of the best, you need to get one or two good, solid waves just to be in the game. And you always need a set as backup, as you have only 45 minutes per heat to work with. If you mess up on your first wave, you'll only have time for one more, and that won't get you through.

Gary reminded me not to risk what you don't need to risk. Just get your two good waves and keep the rest for the final. It's so simple, but it's still some of the best advice I've ever been given.

Detour

The next month came and went, and on 23 December 2009 I received the news that my ex-girlfriend had been diagnosed with a life-threatening illness and needed surgery. It hadn't been that long since we'd broken up, and I felt being with her through this difficult time was the right thing for me to do.

Anyone who has ever had to get a plane ticket from San Francisco to Cape Town over this period will know that, firstly, your chances are rather remote, to say the least, and, secondly, whatever you think you're going to pay, double it. That one-way ticket home cost me all the money I had left, over all three of my bank accounts and overdrafts.

I spent just over a month back home supporting my ex through a difficult time and, by the beginning of February, I realised my dream of surfing the Mavericks Invitational was slipping from my grasp. The contest waiting period would end in two weeks' time, and even if it did run, which was unlikely, I was now so broke after spending all I had to fly home that I didn't know how I could afford to get back over for it. To be honest, right then I was more concerned with how I was going to afford to get through to the end of that week, let alone the month.

Besides being completely broke, I owed a hell of a lot of money on my various credit cards and to my one brother. On 10 February I sat down to look at my finances. I had literally R321 to my name; my overdraft was maxed, my two credit cards were maxed, my savings account was empty.

I was sitting in a sales meeting with my assistant, thinking about how I had got myself into this financial nightmare, how I had literally sacrificed EVERYTHING to get to this point, and for what? And that's when the phone rang.

It was Jeff Clark calling from San Francisco.

"Chris, have you seen the charts? Have you seen that storm coming? There's a strong chance we might be running the Mavericks event! Are you ready? Can you fly out if we call it?"

"Possible, but only if it's called on," I heard myself reply.

I would have to drop everything immediately and be in California within 48 hours. Actually, I would need to be at the airport within two hours and on a plane in four if I was going to make it to the event. Which at that point hadn't even been called.

Trust me, life will always throw you a curve ball when you least expect it. The universe will test you and your resolve to the point of breaking and then beyond, just to see how badly you want it. Are you willing to give it your all, to sacrifice all you have and more to achieve your dreams?

It had taken me 10 long years, almost to the day, to get my shot at the Mavericks title. Ten years of hardship, sacrifice, financial loss and struggle, broken relationships, broken bones, job losses, emotional rollercoasters and a resilient determination to carry on going no matter what, to never give up, to never give in. I had believed with every fibre of my being that I would have my day riding alongside my childhood heroes, my idols and my friends in the Mavericks Invitational.

I was poised on the seesaw of life. Which way would it go?

Coin toss

As soon as I finished my sales meeting I opened the 48-hour forecast. Holy smokes, the storm was massive; it was registering dark purple and grey, which you just don't see on forecasts unless there's a hurricane coming. Except that in this case, the winds looked like they could be light and variable all day ... the event could actually happen!

I got in my car, which was already packed with all my stuff: laptop, warm top, passport, my favourite board, wetsuit and booties. I had everything I needed to head straight to the airport. All that was lacking was the money to buy a ticket. I went to the ATM and pulled up a statement, even though I knew what it would say. Maybe somehow, something had miraculously changed since I looked at it the day before. Unfortunately, it was still exactly the same. I was still completely broke, overdrawn by R49 679 with R321 still available. Awesome.

I called my brother Greg. I already owed him money from the

November trip, but asked if I could borrow another R10 000 to help pay for this ticket. Being Greg, he didn't even hesitate. Okay, well, maybe a little, but he was in.

The ticket cost R15 000, but I felt like I couldn't ask him for any more. So I phoned a really good friend, Andrew Hoeks, and asked whether I could borrow the remaining R5 000.

"For sure, Chris," he said instantly. "Do us proud, brother." (My other brother was overseas, so I couldn't borrow from him, or I surely would have tried!)

When I got to the airport, I called Jeff.

"What's the story, Jeff, are we on? I'm at the airport, my brother is holding the ticket for me. I'm having to borrow the money to pay for it; I'm completely broke. I need to know that we're on. Is the event a go?"

"Chris, we're struggling a bit this side with the new competitor voting system. We need a couple more hours."

"But, Jeff, I don't have a couple more hours. The last flight that's going to get me there in time for the event leaves within the hour. I have to make the call right now. Do I get on the flight or not?"

"Sorry, Chris, all I can say is that it's looking pretty good. It's going to be big, that's for sure, but the wind's a bit ..."

The silence seemed to stretch all the way across the Atlantic, across the United States to the shores of the Pacific and beyond, where the big storm was brewing.

"It's your call," Jeff said. "If you can give me a call in an hour, I'll know for sure."

"Brother, in an hour this flight will be in the air and I will have missed the last plane out to get there in time, and I'll be pretty screwed if you tell me then that it's on and I've missed it."

"It's your call, my friend," Jeff repeated.

I put down the phone. What do I do? I stood there with my board under my arm, wetsuit over my shoulder, and checked the forecast again. It looked like it was going to be massive!

Rationally, it made no sense at all. But so far I had based all my decisions, principles, life lessons, mantras and beliefs on the cornerstone of following my dreams, staying determined and focused, and never giving up. I was in this huge financial dilemma, I was on the brink of committing myself yet again, and with money I didn't have, to get to an event that may not even happen. The thing is, I *believed* it would. I believed with every fibre of my being that the event would be called and that I would make my dream come true. Was I willing to risk it all for my beliefs?

I had about 10 minutes to make the call before my dream would be lost once and for all.

Yes, rationally it made no sense, but I tried to break it down anyway. I had been working towards this moment for the last decade; I had no control over the decision to call the event and there was a 50/50 chance it wouldn't happen; if I got on the plane and it didn't happen, the financial consequences would be devastating, but at least I would never look back and say I never tried, that I never gave it my all, which is what would happen if I *didn't* get on that plane.

I realised then and there that the thing I feared the most, more than anything else in the world, was not taking that risk. The thought of leaving the airport, driving back home and waking up the next morning to find that they had run the event, that I'd had the chance and didn't take it – that was what terrified me the most. I thought to myself, "I never want to be one of those grumpy, bitter old men in a bar talking about how they could have been somebody."

That was it. Screw it. I was all in.

Hiccup

I called Greg and he confirmed and paid for the ticket. There was no going back now. All that was left for me to do was hope and pray they called the event. Or so I thought.

I would only find out what the event organisers had decided when I got to Amsterdam; that's if I had enough time during transit to check my emails. It occurred to me then that I didn't even have enough money to change my ticket in Amsterdam and fly back home should the event not run! I didn't want to think about that right now. I just wanted to get on the plane.

Greg called to say he'd sent me the e-ticket.

"You have about 20 minutes to check in," he said. "I hope you're already in the terminal?"

"I'm walking in with my board under my arm right now," I assured him.

I still had 15 minutes to check in, so I got to the counter and stood in a queue that didn't seem to be moving. After about 10 minutes one of the check-in staff came out from behind the counter and said in a loud voice, "Sorry, ladies and gentleman, this flight is now closed. Unfortunately it has been oversold and it's already full."

What? What was she talking about? Closed? Oversold? I had my ticket in my hand with five people in front of me and another 10 behind me. Suddenly there was pandemonium.

The lady had to shout to be heard above the voices.

"I'm really sorry, but the flight has been oversold by 22 seats. It's totally full, so we've had to close the flight. We will pay for accommodation for people from abroad, and we will be able to get you all on the next flight out to Amsterdam tomorrow. We apologise for the inconvenience."

I was stunned, shocked, paralysed. In over 20 years of travelling I had never been kept off a flight that was overbooked. And now, on the most important flight of my entire life ... You've got to be kidding me!

In a flat panic, I called my brother again. "You won't believe this, bro, the flight is frikkin' oversold. They've just closed it. There

must be something we can do! This is the only flight that will get me there on time. I *have* to get on this flight. I'm going to try to talk to someone, to see if I can get someone to help, but it's chaos here. Can you try to get hold of someone from your side and explain the urgency to them? If I don't get on this flight, I'm going to miss the event! It's that simple. Please see what you can do."

I tried to get to the front to speak to the flight attendant, but frustrated travellers were bombarding her. Even though I tried to explain the urgency, all she could do was repeat that she was sorry, the flight was full, there was nothing she could do.

I stood back and checked the time; the flight would normally be closing for check-in now anyway. Unless my brother could get hold of someone important, I was screwed.

I was just about to give in to despair when Greg called back: "I think I've managed to make a plan. Someone should call for you in the next couple of minutes – let me know if they don't!"

A minute later a woman dressed in very smart attire came out from behind the glass, walked up to the counter and said the sweetest words I have ever heard: "Chris Bertish, is there someone named Chris Bertish here?"

I was up there in a flash. "That's me!"

"I hear you're a Springbok surfer and you're heading to the Olympics of big-wave surfing, is that right?"

"Aaah, yes," I said, trying to sound as confident as possible. I'd never heard it explained like that before, but I guess to people who didn't know any better, that's exactly what it was. At least, that's what my brother must have told someone for this to happen.

"Chris, we have managed to hold the plane for you, but we need to get you through security and customs quickly, so let's go." She told me they were squeezing me onto one of the travelling officer's seats. "So you better do well over there at that event, as I'll be looking in the newspapers for the results!"

She smiled and handed me over to someone else, who escorted me through security.

I found out later that my amazing brother had somehow managed to get through to the air-traffic controllers and convinced them to hold the flight until they could get me on it. Go Bertish!

As I got onto the plane, everyone gave me a round of applause, not because they were happy to see me but because I'd kept everyone waiting for an extra 10 minutes. I just smiled and apologised as I walked down the aisle. I was still blown away, still a little in shock, but I was on the flight and that was all that mattered.

Just before the plane took off I sent the other invitees and the contest director an email:

> Screw rationality. Screw the wind not being perfect. This is the biggest and best swell of the waiting period. We've already missed four swells that we could have run the event on, this is the last two weeks of the waiting period and this is the swell of swells. If you guys don't have the confidence to call the event, I'll call it. This event is going green, it's on! If you need commitment, I'm on the runway in Cape Town, South Africa, my plane is going to take off right after I send this email. I'll see you in the water tomorrow. This event is on. This is Chris signing out.

Amsterdam would be the next moment of truth.

The imperfect storm

I barely had enough time to check my email at Schiphol Airport, but it was long enough to get the news my nerves were on edge to hear: It was a go, we had the green light, the event was on!

I was stoked beyond belief and grinning from ear to ear like a Cheshire cat. But there wasn't any time to celebrate, as I still had

to make the connection. I was home free, we were game on and I was about to live my dream. Or so I thought.

I flew 15 hours across the Atlantic from Amsterdam to Dallas/Fort Worth. And that's where everything started to unravel very quickly.

Fifteen minutes before landing in Dallas, the announcement came over the intercom: "Ladies and gentlemen, due to the severe weather system that's come in from the west, please be prepared for a possibly bumpy landing." Then the part that made my stomach clench: "The airport has been receiving reports of high winds and snow from this severe storm, which has forced numerous flight delays and cancellations. Please check your onward flight details for possible shifts in flight times and schedules."

I had forgotten that there might be a problem with the weather. This was the very storm that was generating the surf I was hoping to ride in the event the next morning, but it was also causing havoc at even the biggest airports with high winds and heavy snowfalls.

But before I could even begin worrying about my next connection, I had to get through passport control. Sometimes the wait at the first port of entry into the US is quick and easy. But on days when you need it to be relatively fast, it's usually the worst nightmare you can possibly imagine.

I tried to remain calm as I watched the minutes, and then hours, pass by, but as my boarding time approached, I started getting edgy and anxious. I had been standing in the queue for two hours and 45 minutes, and I could feel my blood pressure rising. I had 30, then 20, then 15 minutes to get to the departure gate. The possibility of getting to the event on time was becoming slimmer with every second that ticked by. The constant announcements in the background telling passengers to recheck connecting flight times and flight cancellations due to the strengthening storm weren't helping either.

I got through customs with five minutes to spare before the boarding gate closed, but it was on the other side of the terminal, 15 minutes away. Calling on my old track and field skills, I made a run for it.

I arrived at the gate just after they announced the last boarding call. I had just made it!

I smiled at the attendant as I arrived at the gate, flustered and in a heap, and handed over my ticket. She smiled back, scanned my ticket and then frowned.

"Oh, sorry sir, this ticket is not valid for this flight. It seems it hasn't been checked through to your next destination. You need to go back outside to the ticket counter to have it reissued, and then get on the next flight."

"I'm sorry?" I asked in disbelief. I couldn't really compute what she was saying.

"Well, this does happen every now and again with international tickets; they don't get issued all the way through. It should be fine, but you are going to have to go back out of the terminal and speak to American Airlines at the main check-in desk. They'll be able to sort it out for you. I think there's another flight first thing in the morning ..."

By now my internal hard drive was starting to kick into hyper-drive.

"Um, ma'am, I don't think you understand. I *have* to get on this flight."

I started telling her my story, but she put up her hand to stop me right there: "I'm sorry, sir, I need to get these last passengers on board and the flight is about to close. Please step aside ..."

I have to admit that at this point I got stressed and emotional.

"Please," I begged, "you've got to help me! You just *have* to let me on this flight. You don't understand how far I've travelled to get here."

"I'm sorry, sir," she said firmly, "but the flight is full, and we've

got another 10 people on standby before you. You'll just have to wait for the next available flight, like everyone else."

If I missed that flight, I would miss the competition. That would be it; I would be done, finished. It would all be over, everything I had worked towards would be in ruins, including my life, which would be in even more financial turmoil because I would be stuck in America, completely broke and with no options.

I looked down at her nametag. Her name was Grace. I put my hand on her shoulder, looked her straight in the eyes and let it all pour out. All the hard work, the struggles, the setbacks – 10 years of fighting to get to this point. She was probably wondering whether I was deeply passionate or just completely unhinged. Standing in front of her at the boarding gate begging for her help felt pretty desperate, but by this point I had simply lost the ability to care. I would have done anything to get on that plane.

"You don't want to keep me off this flight right now," I pleaded. "Have you watched the movie *The Terminal* with Tom Hanks? I'm so financially broke right now that I'm going to be stuck here, walking your terminal for the next 10 years, stealing Cokes and hamburgers from people because I can't afford to get another plane out of here or change my flight to get back home. If I miss this flight, I miss the event of my life. Please, you've got to help me. Please, really, please."

At some point in my story, something in Grace clicked. I saw a shift in her, and she suddenly softened. She stopped talking past me and looked straight at me. I don't know whether she had some past experience that resonated. Perhaps someone had helped her once when she was stuck in a really tough situation, but I could tell that she finally understood what I was trying to tell her.

"Hold on a second, let me see what I can do. You never know." She went down the tunnel to the plane and came back three minutes later.

"Come on then, I've organised you one of the cabin crew's

spare jump seats. You better do well over there. Now get on quick, before I change my mind!"

Amazing Grace!

A little emotion can go a long way, and meeting the right person on your journey can make all the difference. These pivotal moments are so delicate; so much hangs by a slender thread, and one little decision can change your life forever.

I flopped down into that seat, emotionally and physically drained. I'd been travelling for just over 32 hours and I hadn't slept. I was so stressed and anxious with everything that was happening; I just had to get there, no matter what. So far this had been an emotional rollercoaster from hell, but at least it was over. I was finally on the last plane. I was actually going to make it – I was going to get to San Francisco on time for the start of the event in the early hours of the morning.

What is it they say about not counting your chickens?

The final straw

Eight hours later, I arrived in San Francisco. It was close to midnight local time. I had flown for almost 42 hours and crossed three time zones. I was completely frazzled, a combination of super tired and slightly wired. I just wanted to crash in a bed for 24 hours. But my event was starting in just over six.

I walked over to the baggage carousel and let myself be hypnotised by all the bags going round and round. I was so happy to be there, it was all that mattered. Until, one by one, all the bags were unloaded onto the carousel. Except mine.

No bag, okay, don't stress, it's all good, calm down, I can deal with this. I had the clothes on my back, though now I had no wetsuit, no booties, no warm clothes, no toothbrush, no razor ... but it wasn't a disaster. As long as my surfboards arrived, I would be fine. I had a backup wetsuit and booties stowed at Jeff's place.

I went to the oversized-luggage section and waited for the bag with my two specialised, finely tuned, big-wave gun surfboards, which I had been refining for this exact day for the last 10 years of my life. I watched as the oversized bags came out, and then stopped coming out. A horrible realisation dawned on me.

I found the baggage handler for the area and asked him if there were still more bags to offload, since my surfboards were missing. He just looked at me and sort of laughed.

"Hey, sorry, your bag must have missed the connecting flight. It often happens. Just give us your details and we'll send it over to you in a couple of days when it arrives."

Was he joking? A couple of days? I had just a few *hours* until the most important event of my life. My whole body, mind and soul went into instant panic. Chills ran down my spine and I broke into a cold sweat.

"I've got to surf the biggest international big-wave event on the planet in possibly the biggest and most life-threatening waves in the world, in six hours' time. It's like the Olympics of big-wave surfing," I told him. "I desperately need those boards. They are a seriously specialised piece of equipment. I've been refining these boards for over 10 years for this very day, for this very competition. I. Need. Those. Boards."

He looked at me and said, "Hey, I'm sure it will be okay. Aren't you able to rent one from the beach or something?"

Let me tell you a little bit about those boards.

Knowing your board – the exact weight, shape and feel of it when you are sliding down a wave face of 60 feet – can save your life. It's no exaggeration to say that you are riding on a knife-edge out there, so the precision of a good board, the right board, *your* board and, even more importantly, a board you know well, that you have finely tuned over the years and have practised with count-less times, can mean the difference between life and death.

The boards I had brought over to surf Mavericks in February 2010 were shaped specifically for me by Jeff Clark. When I first met Jeff and he suggested that I try one of his boards, I told him they were really big – remember, I came over to Hawaii for the first time with a 7.10-footer and an 8.8-footer, which were almost two feet smaller than anything anyone was using in those waves. Then I tried one of Jeff's and never looked back. There are probably 12 Clarks in the whole of South Africa today, and 11 of them are in my garage!

Jeff is not only a phenomenal shaper, he is also *the* pioneer of Mavericks. He was the first person to surf there, and surf there alone for 10 years, and shapes boards for those exact conditions. He's not only a master craftsman who knows his art, but he can also see how people ride and then shape boards exactly to suit their particular needs and style.

The first board Jeff gave me was a 9.0 – that was as small as he would go. When he gave it to me, he said, "Chris, if you fall, it's not the board." Now that's a man with a lot of confidence. And he wasn't joking. "If you fall, it's pilot error," he said. "Because the boards are perfect for what they are designed for."

I felt like the Karate Kid being lectured by Mr Miyagi. I only ever fell once on a take-off at Mavericks on that board, and it *wasn't* the board – it really was pilot error. I remember coming in and saying, "You were right, master!"

The first time I took that board out, Jeff came along and watched me from the ski. After my third wave he called me back and made some adjustments.

"I can see you're sticking," he said.

"Yes, it's the board," I replied.

"It's not the board," he said.

He pulled it up on the sled and made some adjustments to the fins and the fin placement and gave it back to me. Suddenly, it

didn't stick any more. There is no other shaper I know who can do that. Jeff knows his boards so well, and he knew me so well, that he could just watch me ride and know exactly what to do to make it perfect.

That was the board that made me realise what it meant to properly ride these big waves. A lot of guys just catch the wave and take off straight, but I could actually *ride* them, as if I were riding smaller waves. Jeff puts a lot of "V" in the tail so that the board really wants to turn. And the rocker line he puts in just fits into the face of the wave better.

That first board I got from Jeff really opened my eyes – it was like I was participating in a different sport. I became a 40 to 60 per cent better surfer. And for the first time I realised how important it is to have the right equipment, how it contributes to the evolution of your ability. It was like being a tennis player going from a wooden racket to a Prince aluminium; like someone from the sixties getting equipment from the nineties. The boards I previously rode were great for other waves, but for Mavericks you need something slightly different.

I had that board for two seasons. Then, in 2006, I got caught inside at Mavericks and snapped it. I went into a complete depression. I still wish I could be riding that board today. You know, like when you have a first love? That's what that board was to me. There was nothing that could compare to it. It had opened my eyes to what was possible. It was like a little treasure, it was my Precious. (No really, I called it my Precious!) So when it broke I had to go away for a few days, because I didn't want to be around anybody. I remember thinking it was like having a beloved pet die.

People don't realise the special relationship big-wave surfers have with their big-wave boards. It's not like you can go and pick out another from the local supermarket. I will never get that exact board ever again. Although you can machine-shape a board with exactly the same measurements, it will still never be the same. The weight, the shape, the rocker line, the way it's glassed, the composition of the foam, the position of the stringer and the wood from which it's made, the exact placement of the fins, the canter ... there are so many variables to try to replicate that it will never be the same. People think that a surfboard is just a surfboard, but they are so wrong. Each one is unique. They are *just* the way they are.

I had tested over and over again the two Clark boards I brought with me to Mavericks in 2010. One of them had all the stickers from my supporters back home. The other was my backup board. Ask any big-wave surfer and they will tell you: never, ever use an unfamiliar board that you've never used before in massive surf, and especially not in a Mavericks Invitational.

But there I was, standing in front of the empty oversized-luggage section at San Francisco International Airport at one o'clock in the morning with some guy telling me to rent a board.

I burst out laughing. Okay, by now I was super tired, more than a little wired and, while I knew there was no point trying to explain it to this guy, I just had to vent my frustration.

"Okay," I said, "you're really not getting it. Imagine I've just arrived at the show-jumping Olympics, and you've lost my horse. I've been training on this horse for years, but you tell me to rent a donkey and compete on that. That's basically what you're telling me!"

I took a deep breath. I was wasting my time and wasn't going to solve anything by carrying on as I was. So I left my details and headed out to meet up with my ride.

It was just after 1:30 a.m. and Jeff's son Kevin was there to pick me up. We drove back to Jeff's place. By the time we arrived I was physically, emotionally and mentally drained. I literally flopped down on the bed.

But I had all sorts of thoughts running through my head. This was hardly ideal preparation for the contest of my life. I'd had virtually no sleep. I hadn't been able to eat properly on the plane. I didn't have my key equipment – thank goodness I'd left a backup wetsuit and booties at Jeff's for exactly this possibility. But without my favourite boards, it felt like a recipe for disaster.

I needed to clear my head, calm down, let go of all the negative thoughts and focus on the positives. I lay in bed and tried to slow everything down. Just breathe and focus. As usual, I started visualising the waves and how I was going to ride them in the competition in a couple of hours, even though my mind just wanted to shut down.

I could see myself taking off on this huge wave. But, as had happened with Jaws, I got halfway down the face and hit a bump. And fell.

I couldn't go to sleep until I'd replayed the scenario over and over in my head, until I'd managed to work out how I was going to get over and through that bump in the wave, which was bigger than normal, almost like a mini step – bearing in mind that a mini step in a 60-foot wave is like a four-foot wave in the face of the bigger wave, which can act like a ramp as you try to get over it. In my mind I kept falling after dropping over that ledge. I figured out that if I managed to stay flexible and agile, like Elastoman, and not go stiff the way so many do in a situation when they are about to fall, I could almost wiggle and contort my body through it.

In my mind I practised unravelling like a coil, using my body as a shock absorber, keeping my balance even as I went off-balance, and not falling off. I focused on this until I finally saw myself coming through it and making the drop. Only once it was done, only when I could visualise that, could I finally drift off to sleep. The lights went out and my mind shut down. Blackout.

8

Epic!

It felt like minutes later that Jeff was gently shaking my shoulder.

"Chris, you gotta get up, bud, it's time. The waves are giant and the event's going to be starting soon. You need to get your stuff together and get down there."

I had slept for three hours.

Jeff lent me one of his backup boards in the garage. "It's very similar to yours, same rocker, a little longer, at 9.2, but it'll be perfect." I didn't know it at the time, but that little bit of extra length would help me that day more than I could have possibly predicted.

If anybody knew what board would work for me, it was Jeff. It may not have been the exact board I had been practising on, the board that I knew like the back of my hand, but it was pretty close and he'd shaped it, so it would have to be good enough.

I had woken up strangely calm. Somewhere in my mind I had a sense that I had done everything in my power to get to this point, and whatever happened after was up to fate. I knew I would give it everything I had; the rest was written in the stars.

We try to control every aspect of our lives, and so often we're in circumstances beyond our control. There comes a time when you just have to sit back and, as hard as it may be at the time, accept

that whatever happens, happens; that that's how it is meant to be. Just let it go and let it flow, don't fight it.

I prepped my new board. I had made extra stickers with the names of all the people who had contributed to getting me there, and I stuck those up and down the top rails and nose of the board. That really helped to ground me, calm me further and remind me of everything that had gone into getting me there, and all the people who had helped me and believed in me along the way.

As I bent down to pick it up, a last random sticker fell out onto the deck of my board. It read: "Chris would go!"

It was a send-up of the "Eddie would go!" slogan, which referred to the famous Hawaiian waterman Eddie Aikau, who would take any wave once he had committed to it. Eddie never hesitated; once he started paddling, Eddie would always go! Eddie was lost at sea in 1978 trying to save a whole lot of people in a storm. He swam towards shore to summon help and was never seen again. It's a testament to his memory that, when hesitating in the face of a great challenge, the Hui spur one another on by saying, "Eddie would go!"

That sticker was a reminder that no matter what happened, no matter how fierce and how big the waves I was about to face that day, just like Eddie, I would go.

I took the "Chris would go!" sticker and stuck it separately from the others, right in the centre of my board, two feet from the nose, along the middle stringer. It would be in front of my face while I was paddling, exactly where I would look before getting to my feet. Pure inspiration.

It was my day and, no matter what happened, I would not hold back. Today was about giving it everything, down to the last drop, to the very last breath.

Little did I know it would require exactly that, and more.

Tsunami

At 7 a.m. it was barely light and Half Moon Bay was jam-packed with thousands of people, bustling with the frenzy of the impending event. I overheard a couple of the safety guys talking about the size of the swell out there, and started to feel a bit nervous and edgy. But it was the booming sounds I could hear far off in the distance that really got the butterflies going in my stomach. The waves were breaking on the reef, more than four kilometres away. It had begun.

I pulled my backup wetsuit up to my waist, put on my warm K-Way down jacket, pulled a knitted beanie over my head and put my headphones on so that Pearl Jam and Nickelback could help me get into the right headspace. I pulled my equipment out of the car, took a deep breath, looked down at my borrowed Clark surfboard with all the names from home on it and the "Chris would go" sticker, and smiled. This was it, I was finally here, I had made it. I was about to live my lifelong dream.

I walked down the path to Pillar Point and the beach at the end of the breakwater, where the event site was set up. People were flocking in from all directions and it was extremely difficult to drown out everything around me and just focus on my music, slow things down in my head and get into the zone. *Delete everything around you, calm, just calm, and slow things down, focus, you can do this,* I told myself. *All there is, is 100 per cent complete calm, focused space. You can do this.*

Music was blaring and public announcements were being made over a PA system. A 50-foot Jumbotron screen had been erected to show the live action and scaffolding had been put up for the commentators. There were tents and gazebos all over the event site, and scaffolding also lined the beach. It was like a circus.

But that wasn't what scared me. What really scared me were the waves that I saw on the other side of the Boneyard – that jagged

157

array of protruding rocks sticking up over 20 feet, just waiting to greet your slightest miscalculation. Massive white water unloaded and smashed up against the rocks, and the waves that broke out at the back peak seemed to be breaking in a place I hadn't seen in the 10 years I'd been surfing there. Something was different; the waves were breaking in proper slow motion. Boooom! That only meant one thing – the surf was *ginormous*! The waves detonated on the reef with a size and magnitude I had never seen before. I didn't know it yet, but they were, in fact, the biggest paddle-in waves in the history of the event and the sport. Bigger than anything anyone had ever seen or paddle-surfed before.

As I was standing there, just trying to settle and focus my mind on the event, a huge wave came rushing up the beach and slammed into the breakwater where many of the spectators were standing. It smashed up against and over the wall, knocking about 40 people completely off their feet and battering the webcasting tower, washing people, stalls and customers through the event site and out into the lagoon.

It was like slow motion in a disaster movie. Suddenly I was running into the chaos, Pearl Jam in my headphones, torrents of water flowing through the entire site, trying to drag people to safety. I grabbed a woman out of the water and put her over one shoulder. I hauled a kid over the other shoulder just as water rushed past and all around me. This wasn't quite how I'd pictured preparing for the scariest and most important event of my life.

I had to get off the land and out into the ocean, my church, my sanctuary, away from the circus, the clutter and the mayhem. I called Jeff, who was out on the water on the ski, and asked him to come pick me up. Strange as it may seem, I felt like the only place that was safe and that would ground me was out in the heaving ocean.

Driving out there on the back of the ski with Jeff was pretty special. I had dreamt of this day for over a decade, and now it was here. Except it seemed a little surreal, as the waves looked so exponentially bigger than anything we had ever seen out there before. I asked Jeff about the conditions out back, and the look on his face really had me worried; even he looked concerned, and that literally never happens!

These waves were on a whole different level. I think it's safe to say that everyone competing out there was more than scared that day; it was truly terrifying.

We pulled up into the channel and watched one of the first main sets of the day march in, stand up like some sort of mutant monster, and unload and detonate on the reef. It was like watching liquid mountains travelling in and exploding in slow motion. Over 60 feet of raw Pacific open-ocean power; maybe more – it was hard to tell.

Then it was time for my heat. One of the officials handed me my orange contest vest – this was it, I finally had the prestigious Mavericks Invitational vest in my hands! Just before I climbed off the ski with my board, I gave Jeff a huge hug. Then I looked him straight in the eye, to thank him for more than I could put into words, and gave him a high five. An amazing calm came over me. Yes, it was big. Bigger than anything I'd seen or surfed in my life before. But as I sat there and splashed water in my face and pulled that contest vest over my head, I realised that I was really there. I was finally in the Mavericks Big Wave Invitational. I had made it.

BOOOOM!

The horn went to start the heat. We had 45 minutes to make our mark.

It was game on.

I paddled out into a line-up that looked like a crazy scene of

turbulent destruction. The ocean was menacing, dark and ominous, with massive amounts of water moving around to make a volatile and unpredictable playing field. I had surfed this spot so many times over the past decade, but on this day it didn't look like anything I had ever seen before. All my usual line-up points and markers went straight out the window. This was anyone's game. It was going to be a day of clever planning and strategising. But, above all, it was going to be about pure survival!

There were six surfers in each of the four starting heats. Half would drop out after the first round, leaving 12 surfers in the semis and six in the final.

For the first five minutes of our first heat, my five fellow competitors and I just tried to find our places in the line-up. It all looked so foreign with the waves peaking and breaking in abnormal places, and we were all just trying the best we could to make sense of it all and not get caught inside.

After five minutes the horizon suddenly disappeared and I began to stress, as I saw the first big set starting to form. It looked different in that it was huge. I let the first couple of waves go, just to be safe, hoping that the other guys would go on the first two, which would put them out of place for the third and fourth – if there were that many.

As I came over the second, the third was waiting for me. The other guys had paddled for the second wave, leaving this one wide open. There was only one other surfer paddling on my outside, but I knew he'd have to give me right of way, because I was deeper. I put my head down and started paddling. Number three wasn't as big as the first two, but it was still a mountain of water, big enough to call a monster ... I gave it 100 per cent. My timing and positioning were good – I was in.

Within an instant I was on my feet, looking straight into the eye of the monster. I reminded myself to stay low and focus on making the drop and getting out onto the shoulder – the safe zone. I managed the drop and negotiated the bump. I could tell immediately that there was a lot more speed with the power and energy of this swell, which was breaking in the 21-second period range. I managed to make the bottom turn and made it out onto the open face and then onto the shoulder and into the channel. Wave one, done, under my belt. I gave a sigh of relief – the pressure was off. It can be done, they can be ridden; it's just about being clever and finding the right waves.

I paddled back past a hooting and cheering line-up of support boats out in the channel. The energy in the water was intense and amazing and insane, all at the same time. I headed towards the horizon and looked to sit further out than usual, by a good 150 metres, which is significant ... and that's when I saw the bump on the horizon.

Then the horizon disappeared altogether. Something big was coming. I looked around to see where I was in the line-up. I figured that because I was further out I was probably in the safe zone – but then again, was there a safe zone on a day like today?

I slowly started paddling further out. I looked around and saw all the guys scratching for the back line. We all knew what was coming, but none of us expected what was about to arrive. As we paddled over the first wave, we heard everyone hooting and whistling from the channel, which normally means there's something scary coming that the competitors are not able to see. I dug deep and got over the first one along with two other guys, and that's when we saw the behemoth right behind it.

The horizon was obscured by a really big slab of ocean, developing like nothing I had seen before. I started paddling faster to get out and over it, but all the time I kept thinking, *Holy smokes, that is the biggest wall of water I have ever seen! But there's no way a wave could possibly break this far out.*

Three seconds later it became clear that this beast was starting to stack up across the entire line-up, over 400 metres wide, and much faster than I had thought possible. It was just getting bigger and bigger and higher and higher and that's when the realisation hit me: *Holy shit, this thing is going to break literally 20 feet in front of me and I'm about to get caught inside. Caught inside by the biggest, scariest wave I have ever seen, all within the first 10 minutes of my first heat. What the hell did I do to deserve this?* I knew I was in a whole lot of trouble. This could actually be the end of the road.

Everything went into slow motion, including my thoughts, as I ditched my board and prepared to dive under the wave. I remember thinking, *Okay, calm down, focus, you can get through this, you've trained for this, you are a machine, this exact moment is what all the training was for. You might be able to get under the lip and come up through the other side, and get one breath before it pulls you back down ... calm down, calm down, you might get under it ...*

I knew it was going to be bad, and I also knew that those of us who got caught by this and anything behind it were in deep, deep trouble; this wave was in excess of 20 to 25 metres (that's 65 to 70 feet) high. It looked like it had drawn the entire ocean into itself, and we were in the worst possible place you could be, just in front of the apex of the wave, where it was about to unload its most intense, ferocious power, equalling about 600 cubic tons of terror, directly onto our heads.

I tried to dive under it, but I knew it probably wasn't going to work out favourably this time. I braced for impact; that horrible feeling when you know what's coming and there is nothing you can do about it, other than just wait for it. I knew deep down I was caught. I heard as much as felt it hit me like a 10-ton truck: BOOOOM!

It was the loudest and most frightening crack I have ever heard, like a thunderclap right next to my ear. At the same instant the whole world shook violently. It felt like a massive underwater earthquake. Just before it gripped me, everything went black as the ocean unleashed all its ferocity on my head, sending me 30 feet straight down in a split second, to the point where my eardrums almost burst. I tried to equalise as I plummeted downwards, but it felt like Poseidon himself was trying to rip my arms and legs from my body.

My ankle was still attached to my board via my leash, and I was instantly ripped sideways and then dragged backwards by my one leg, underwater in sheer blackness, for almost a kilometre – that's 10 football fields – at a speed twice as fast as an Olympic sprinter. It felt as if I had been shut in a tiny box with Mike Tyson, Bruce Lee and eight ninja warriors, all punching and kicking the living crap out of me at the same time, while I was trying to remain calm, thinking of white fluffy clouds, working through the colours of the rainbow and not taking a breath – no matter how much my body was screaming at me to do so.

Don't fight it, don't fight it, just go with the flow ... Relax; when you fight it, you use more oxygen; relax, breathe inside your head, slow it down.

I did that until I wasn't able to flow with it any longer; I just needed to get to the surface. But at this point I was actually getting pushed down even deeper. If I carried on going I would go over what's known at Mavericks as "the Waterfall"; an underwater shelf at the edge of the main reef where it drops another 20 feet. Just as I was thinking about it, I felt myself go almost weightless as I dropped another four to five metres, over the ledge, to a much colder, pitch-black, oily, slow-moving space.

It was almost eerily quiet down there, below the turbulence and turmoil of the angry ocean above. That's when I knew I was in a really bad place. If I didn't make a plan quickly, no matter how fit and trained and prepared I was, I would not come up alive.

Another 15 to 20 seconds and I would black out; 30 seconds after that my epiglottis would open, water would rush into my body and I would start drifting lifeless along the ocean's flow; another four minutes and I would be clinically dead, beyond help or recovery. It had happened to a couple of the best big-wave Hawaiians over the years – Mark Foo and Sion Milosky – and had almost happened to Shane Dorian and Greg Long.

If I wanted to survive, I had just seconds to get out of that dark and dangerous place. As I bent down to grab my leash so I could use it to guide me to the surface, I heard the sound every big-wave surfer dreads: the rumble of the next wave passing over my head. This is when you know you are in serious trouble, as you are still a long way off being able to get to the surface to take a breath. Some people don't survive two-wave hold-downs; no one we know of has ever survived a three-wave hold-down. I had about 15 seconds to make it to the surface.

I grabbed my leash, thanking God that it hadn't snapped with the pressure, and with the last bit of energy I could wrench from my oxygen-deprived muscles, I started climbing it to my 9.2-foot polyurethane board, which would have been floating like a cork on the surface.

Except that my leash, which is normally 12 feet long, had been stretched to 20 feet and was straining to the point of almost giving way. I prayed that it wouldn't snap before I got to my board, because I could feel my body starting to shut down. The feeling is actually quite pleasant: everything becomes less of a struggle and a nice, calm sensation comes over you. That's when you know you're about to black out. I got to the tail of my board and pulled myself up to the midpoint – and that's when I realised I was still underwater!

Now I had to make a very quick decision: try to stay conscious and hold onto my board until it eventually got to the surface –

where it should have been already – or ditch my board and try with everything I had left, which was basically nothing, to swim to the surface before my body shut down. I started to drift into that comfortable place with the little black dots when, suddenly, the brightest light opened up above me. I had hit the surface. My face popped up and I managed one huge gasp of air just as I turned to see the next 40-foot wall of white water and Pacific power bearing down on me. I didn't have time to dive down, and it smashed straight into me with such force that it almost knocked that one precious breath right out of me.

And so the spin cycle began again. I knew I was in serious trouble; unless this 40-foot wall of turbulence and power let me up easily, I wasn't going to survive. I sort of just let go inside; I had no more energy left and I didn't want to try to fight it. I just hoped with all my heart that it would let me go and let me get to the surface quickly.

But I wasn't that lucky. After what seemed like forever, I started swimming upwards, but there was so much aerated water that it was almost impossible. I was beginning to feel like there was no hope left. Then my head broke the surface. I gasped, took in some foamy water, spluttered and looked around for the rescue ski. But they couldn't get in to help me, because there was too much turbulence and aerated water, and not enough time to get to me before the next wall of white water hit me again.

And that was it. The next wave got me and I was back down again, but this time with literally nothing left in my tank. I could feel my body succumbing to a weird, slow numbness, but I managed to claw my way back to the surface and the intense light once again. As I was slipping out of consciousness, I saw a ski out of the corner of my eye coming to get me. It was coming in fast and I knew I needed to do two critical things. My mind was still trying to keep me alive. *Think rationally*, I started to coach myself. *Stay with me, stay with me.*

First, I bent down to rip the leash off my leg so that my board wouldn't tombstone behind me and drag me back into the ocean if the rescue operator managed to pick me up. Second, I tried to keep one hand above the surface for a few more seconds so he could see me and haul me out of the water onto the back of the rescue sled before the next 30 feet of white water chased us down and engulfed us. He was going to have to be extremely quick to get us both out of the danger zone and into the safety of the channel on the side.

As simple as those two tasks might sound reading them now, they were possibly the two most difficult things I have ever had to do in my life. It took me two fatigued attempts to release myself from the leash, and once I was free I was completely helpless and at the mercy of the sea, as I had just severed my one and only lifeline to the surface. I grabbed a foamy breath among the six-inch layer of foam on the surface, just to make an already life-threatening situation even worse. I felt my head starting to slip back underwater and just managed to keep my hand up above the surface so the rescue operator could still see me. Just before I went under I saw him. He was 15 metres away, coming in fast, but the next wave was bearing down on us at speed. I could feel myself starting to sink. I commanded my other arm and my legs to pull and kick, to keep me at the surface, but they refused to obey. I was slipping beneath the water and I had no way of getting myself back up. My body was shutting down.

I felt someone grab my hand and, with adrenaline-fuelled super strength, haul me out of the water and onto the back of the sled. The guy held me by one arm and I vaguely heard him shout, "Hold on, hold on!"

The next white-water wall exploded behind us as he throttled up and got the ski back on a plane to get out of the impact zone. The towering 30-foot wave started to engulf us from behind, and the ski struggled to gain traction in the turbulent, aerated water.

For a second, the white water engulfed the back of the ski. Even in my semi-conscious state I knew that if it got both of us on the ski, I would definitely drown.

But somehow we came bouncing out in front of the booming mass of white water. The rescue operator (I would later discover was Frank Quirarte) reached back and grabbed me just as I was about to slip off the ski. He kept on telling me to hold on, but it was the one thing I could not do. I couldn't use my arms, I couldn't use my legs, I could barely breathe. I was slipping in and out of consciousness and everything was a blur.

Frank whisked me into the channel and started shouting at me again: "Do you want me to take you to the paramedics?"

I tried with all my might just to get my head up to answer him, but nothing would come out, not even a simple yes or no, no matter how hard I tried. My brain, unbeknown to me at the time, was systematically shutting down functions in order of hierarchical importance, so that it could focus on the single most important thing it needed to do in order to sustain life: breathe!

We were on the shoulder now, out of the impact zone, by the rocks that I had just been flushed through underwater. I lay on the sled thinking, *That's it, it's over, I'm done. Oh my God, I actually survived that! I'm actually still alive!* But even while I was telling myself I was done, a little voice was already asking, *Is this how it's really going to end? After everything I've done? After everything I've sacrificed to get here?*

As we moved slowly out along the channel, although my head was still down on the side of the rescue sled, I began to get feeling back in my limbs. I was almost starting to breathe normally again, even though my body felt like lead, drained to the point of complete depletion. But something in my mind shifted as I started to think clearly again. If I could get through this and survive, there was still hope.

I still had the ability to choose my path, to make a decision. I could give up and throw in the towel, or I could carry on going. I had survived, I was conscious and there was still time left on the clock.

I live my life according to one simple philosophy: when I'm faced with a choice, I ask myself, "If I had the opportunity to do this again at another time, would I make the same choice?" I know that as long as I give it my all, every single time, I will always be happy. So, while I was lying on the rescue sled, I already knew that no matter how physically exhausted, battered and bruised I felt, I still had a choice. I thought about Frank's question and realised that the answer was quite simple. I was still alive – traumatised, but alive – and even though my body wasn't operating at any-where near full capacity, all my basic functions were starting to work again.

So I asked myself, "How will I feel looking back on this situation 10 years from now? Will I wonder what could have happened if only I'd tried?"

I was reminded of a picture that used to hang in my dad's office and now hangs in mine. You may have seen it before: it's a picture of a stork eating a frog. The frog is halfway down the stork's throat, but his little arms are sticking out from the side of the stork's beak and he's throttling the stork. The caption under-neath it reads: "Never, ever, ever give up!"

Whatever motivates you to carry on, no matter what it is, you need to cling to it and use it to keep you going when times get tough. That picture has always motivated me, and the memory of it inspired me again now.

I looked up at Frank and said, "Don't take me to the para-medics. Take me back ... take me back to the backup boards in the channel."

By the time we got out to where the boards were attached to

a buoy in the calm water of the channel, I knew I was going to be okay, even though I felt like I was made of lead, just trying to pull myself upright on the back of the ski.

Frank dropped me off and headed back to his rescue work, as another set had come in. I just lay in the water holding my board alongside me, floating with the help of the buoyancy of my wetsuit. I just needed five minutes to regain my composure, to process everything as the heat wound down into its last minutes.

I thought about everything that had got me to this day, this hour, this very second. I was here, living the dream I had envisioned for myself, but it was very different to how I had imagined it yesterday, or even half an hour before. I could paddle back to the boat like everyone would expect me to do right now, and call it a day. I would be done, the dream would be over and everyone would understand and pat me on my back and say well done, I don't know how you got through that situation, it's amazing you're still alive.

That was one choice, but it would mean I would sit the rest of the day recovering on the boat watching everyone else living *my* dream. I would have to get on a plane and go back home, where everything would be the same, the work, the debt, the struggles. I could live with that, as long as I knew I had given it absolutely EVERYTHING I had, until there was nothing left.

The thing is, I was still alive, I could still function, and so, in theory, I still had a little bit left. I hadn't given it everything. Not yet.

I had another choice. I could get back on my board for the last eight minutes of the heat and try with everything I had left to paddle back out, no matter how long it took. Whether I caught a wave or not was immaterial; what mattered was that I would never be able to look back at the situation in the days, months and years to come and say I didn't give it my absolute all. Every

last drop. In that one moment, it became crystal clear that I had to give it a shot, no matter the outcome. It didn't matter: win or lose, wave or no wave. What mattered was that I went out swinging!

I pulled myself up onto my backup board and just flopped over it, arms hanging down off the sides. Even that simple task felt like a huge ask. I lay there for a minute collecting myself and my strength, then I brought one arm up onto the board to check the time remaining in the heat: 7 minutes and 23 seconds.

I looked up at where I needed to go, and with all the effort and energy I had I took that first stroke. *There, you see, it can be done,* I thought to myself. *Just one stroke at a time.* Normally it would have taken me just over two minutes to get to the back line, but every stroke was a mammoth undertaking. I didn't even want to get back out to where everyone was sitting; I was too exhausted to wait for waves in the same place as them, and I couldn't risk getting caught inside by another one. I knew I wouldn't survive that. I just wanted to get out onto the side of the channel before the heat ended. If, by some miracle, a wave came to me in the last minutes or seconds of the heat, I would try to flop down to catch it and would give it my all.

I got to where I felt comfortable and sat up on my board to regain my breath. I looked down at the time remaining: 1 minute and 45 seconds. Okay, I guess I was done; that was surely it. But at least I had made it out to the back and I could never say I didn't try.

As I was thinking that, I noticed a big bump on the horizon. It was a proper set, and it looked like it was forming up pretty quickly. I wasn't moving from my place by the side of the channel; I simply didn't have enough energy to get to the zone where the other guys were sitting. I just watched and waited as the set started to build. Just over a minute later, the first wave came thundering through. I watched one of the guys catch the second and two catch the third. By the time the fourth one came into view there was less than 30 seconds remaining on the clock.

But this wave was different. It was coming in at a totally different angle to the others and wasn't going to break in the same place. Hold on a second – it was swinging *way* wide and looked like it was going to come right towards me off the side of the channel. I couldn't believe my eyes. I was struck with fear, but I also thought, *What are the chances of that happening?* And the wave looked perfect, not too big, not too scary, and coming right at me. I just had to turn, paddle and catch it, with literally 20 seconds remaining in the heat and zero energy left in the tank.

If I fell, I would be dead, that was for sure. My body couldn't take another beating. I didn't even have the strength to paddle for the wave. All I could do was take one last look back, swivel my board around, flop down and wait until I felt the wave start to lift me from behind. Then I would use all the energy I could muster and take one last stroke with both my arms at the same time – something I had not done before or since; you normally require a lot more paddling, but that's all I had left in me, just one big, solid stroke.

By chance, fate, destiny – whatever you want to call it – I suddenly felt the wave picking me up. Holy smokes, I was actually in!

I was so shocked that I almost tripped over my fatigued feet just trying to stand up on the board. Then I was up. *Stay low, stay low, absorb the bump, don't fall, you're not going to fall, you're not going to fall*, I kept repeating to myself as I dropped down to the bottom and angled my board away off the side of the wave and into the channel and the safe zone. The wave exploded behind me. I had done it. I had actually caught a wave, more by chance than anything else. I flopped off the side of my board into the channel, just as the buzzer from the siren sounded behind me.

I had done it. Win or lose, I had survived and given it my all and I could go home happy, content and with no regrets. I had survived the biggest waves ever at Mavericks and lived my dream, and no one could ever take that away from me.

What you wish for

"That was heavy, my friend!" Jeff said as he pulled his ski up to the support boats to collect me. "Everyone was freaking out in the channel. That wave that landed on your head was frikkin' huge!"

"I'm just stoked everyone's alive and safe," I told him, after establishing that no one had, in fact, drowned out there. "But Clarkman, I'm done. I have nothing left. I'm so glad it's over."

I'll never forget the look he gave me. "Done? I'm not so sure, bud. You may have made it through that heat in third place. I think only three of you out there caught two waves."

You'd think I would have been over the moon, considering that I might be advancing to the semi-finals, but the thought was terrifying. I didn't know how the hell I would be able to go back out there. The waves were getting bigger and bigger with each set that came in.

"Clarkman," I said, feeling a little desperate, looking out into the heaving line-up, "I don't know if I can go back out there again. I've never come so close to drowning. I am so physically drained, I don't think I'll survive another beating."

"Hold on a second," he said. "I've got exactly what you need."

He opened the front lid of the jet ski and rummaged around like a mad scientist, then pulled out a bag of energy bars and two sachets of Clif glucose.

"Take two of these, my friend. Pure glucose, pure energy, straight into your system."

I tore off the tops, squeezed both into my mouth and hoped he was right. To go back out there in 30 minutes in the state I was in would have been suicidal.

Luckily the Clarkman is always right; within 30 seconds I could feel the energy returning to my body, like a flat battery recharging. Maybe I could do this. I got to my own little bag of tricks and pulled out two bananas, some chewy Clif energy bars and a bottle of water, and consumed them all in the space of two and a half minutes. I was putting my warm jacket on over my wetsuit when they announced the results of my heat. I was still half hoping I hadn't made it through, still struggling with the prospect of going back out into an environment that had just almost killed me.

They announced Anthony Tashnick and Kenny "Skindog" Collins in first and second place, and then the words I was dreading: "And also making it through to the semis, Chris Bertish in third place. Congratulations, gentlemen! Please start getting ready; you'll be going back in after the next quarter-final in 45 minutes' time."

It wasn't what I was hoping or expecting. But I had just had something to eat, my energy levels were reviving and I was starting to feel a bit better. Who knew how I would feel in another 10 or 20 minutes? The anticipatory adrenaline was already starting to surge through my system. What I needed to do now was work on my mental state if I was going to get through this alive.

I closed my eyes, slowed everything down, blanked out everything else around me and just focused on my breathing and my thoughts. I ran through all my reasons for being there, the lifelong dream, the hard work, the sacrifices ... I thought of the people back home counting on me to give it my best. Then I asked myself the hardest question of all: "Do you believe you can do it?"

The answer came quickly: *I'm not sure if I can right now, but I'm going to give it everything, 110 per cent, no matter what. And whatever happens afterwards is up to fate!*

Life is all about choices. It's the decisions in the hard times, not

the easy times, which define you. There's no such thing as luck in life – you make your own.

Back into the chaos

I think we all had a sense that there was something special, something monumental, happening in the ocean that day. I felt like a gladiator as I pulled my contest singlet back over my head, splashed cold water onto my face, closed my eyes, focused on the task ahead and sank down onto my board to take those first couple of strokes towards the line-up, ready for battle. Gladiators ready, here we go ... Game on!

It was a new heat and I had to start mentally fresh: clean the slate, let go of everything that had happened in the past two hours – except for the lessons I had learnt. I had to use those and apply them to the next three hours. I had to change my game plan, push the reset button and move forward with a revised strategy in order to get through the next heat. After that I could relook, reassess and readjust if I had to.

This time I would try to be smarter and have a safer, more strategic game plan. I wanted to prevent repeating what had happened in my first heat. Now, more than ever, it was a game of survival, as the swell continued to build and everyone there knew they were witnessing something very special.

My new objective and game plan: two medium-sized waves, much more calculated, good positioning, not too late, no great risks, nothing crazy.

My number-one priority: survival – don't get caught inside, whatever happens.

Being clear about what I needed to do out there was one thing, but as I paddled out into the line-up I realised that achieving it in this deadly and volatile environment was a whole different story.

In these conditions, very little is within your control. Everything you know pretty much goes out the window. You have to be reactive to the conditions in order to survive, but proactive in your strategy to thrive!

The first set came only 10 minutes into the heat. I let the first two waves go; I wanted to take my time to thin out the competitors and give myself more room to move and more options to work with. I was looking for a medium-sized wave and less pressure from the other competitors, who would be hassling me into a place I didn't want to be. I didn't want to be forced too deep or too late, not today. (A medium-sized wave on this day was like the biggest wave of the day at any of the big-wave spots around the world, just heavier and scarier, because it's Mavericks, after all!)

I came over the second wave and the third looked good; big, but not ginormous; manageable and pretty readable. I was in the right place, with only one other competitor on my outside. As I was deeper, I had priority. I gave a quick yell to the right – "Ooooye!" – and looked around again to see it building behind me. I could get this, I was just on the corner of the apex, my positioning was perfect, my timing was good – this was a good wave.

I put my head down and gave it all the effort and pull I could. I needed this wave. I took two extra strokes and felt the glide. I was up in a split second and dropping in steep, deep and later than I thought, but on the perfect line down to the bottom. Driving down off the bottom and up into the pocket, I headed straight up onto a higher line and onto the shoulder. I carved back into the power pocket on the shoulder of the wave and pulled out off the back into the channel. Job well done. Nice, Bertish. A perfect start, a clinical first wave, awesome. I was on the scoreboard. One down and one to go!

I paddled back out. *Okay, I've got this, I can do this, I can pull this off*, I said to myself. *Just stick to the game plan*. I had another 30 minutes to get my next wave and then I would be done.

I got back out just as the next set came in. I went up and over the first one, as big-wave world champ Carlos Burle dropped super late into a big one. Wow, scary and unbelievable. The guy was my childhood hero – they don't call him "the Jackal" for nothing. Precise, clinical and professional, he's a superb athlete and goes on almost anything.

I paddled slightly wider and up and over the second and third. There was a slightly smaller fourth wave, which I thought I could possibly get. I turned and paddled, but then realised at the last minute that I was too late and rushing it. I pulled back: focus, no rushing. I turned my board and went to find a place to wait for the next set to rear its ugly head.

Ten minutes later we all saw another set on the horizon. The other guys were all out back, jostling for position so they could be in the right place, pushing one another deeper and later. I didn't want any part of that, so I swung my board over and paddled wider, towards the third wave of the set, thinking I could get out in time to swivel for this bigger one and go. I was spot on. The others were too deep for the third as they'd paddled for the second. I turned, put my head down and started stroking as hard as I could to build my speed to catch it.

The wave started to build really quickly and began lurching out under me. I knew it wasn't worth it, so I pulled back off the top and stopped paddling. Because of this, I missed the smaller one behind it, which Skinny Collins caught. Damn, I thought I had that one! Now I was exactly where I didn't want to be: I had missed the last two sets, and if I wanted to get into the final, I would have to go on one of the waves in the next set, like it or not. Time was winding down and I'd only had one wave. I knew that Carlos, Skinny and Anthony had all had two waves; Nathan Fletcher and I were one wave short.

In these kinds of conditions it's amazing how you can go from being ahead in the game to being on the back foot in such a short space of time. Maybe I was rattled because I'd started over-thinking things. Maybe that was why I was pulling back. It's never good to start thinking too much while you're out there; your mind will play tricks on you and your thoughts will run away with you. You really have to stay positive, stay focused and keep your head together. If you let your thoughts stray from the positive to the negative, they'll start trying to talk you down and out of what you are trying to achieve.

You just need the right last wave and you're done, I reminded myself. *C'mon, bud, don't be stupid, you can do this. Breathe, focus, just get through this heat in one piece. You can do this ... just one more wave. You've done this all before, every time you've been out here.*

I looked at the countdown on my watch: under five minutes remaining. There was definitely time for one decent last set before the end of the heat, and I knew that when it came, one of those waves was mine. I wanted to make that final, and if I played my cards right, I could do it. Just one more wave!

I was mentally mentoring myself with one eye on the horizon, which was starting to change and shift. A big black mark was rising in the distance. The people on the support boats started to holler and whistle. We were in for a huge set and I was a little worried about getting caught like last time.

My heart was pounding in my throat as we all paddled over the first wave, almost next to one another in the line-up. I was in the middle as we came over the top of the first one. Two of the guys swung to try to go for the second, while Carlos, Skinny and I paddled over it to see if there was a third and fourth waiting on the other side. It was such a huge, powerful and solid set, and there seemed to be at least three or four waves in each big set now, so we all had a feeling there would be more.

As we came over the second, we immediately saw the third, and it was a monster. It was at least 50 to 60 feet of open-ocean, raw Pacific power, like a liquid mountain coming at us at high speed,

but so big it looked like it was moving in slow motion. It seemed to be holding back just enough so that we weren't out of place, even though we were all frantically paddling to get over and away from it.

That's when it happened: Carlos stopped paddling on my outside and started swivelling his board around, like he was turning to go. In an instant, I knew: if there wasn't a fourth wave behind this one, I was out, that would be the end of my Mavericks dream. There wasn't enough time left for another set, so this was it.

There are very few moments in life that really matter, that challenge you to test yourself and risk it all. For me, right here, right now, this was one of those moments, the moment I had been working towards all my life. I was deeper than Carlos and five feet on his inside, and therefore had right of way. I had to go. I knew if I didn't, he would, and he'd most certainly get through and win the heat.

Screw the game plan, this was it. Either I was all in, or it was all over.

I swivelled my board on a dime – something guys on bigger boards aren't able to do – put my head down and started paddling as if my life depended on it (in this situation, it actually did). By now I was paddling next to Carlos, but he was already slightly ahead and up to speed. The wave just got bigger and bigger as it rose up behind us. Holy shit, this thing was going to be huge! *I'm still going, whatever happens. I'm in, I'm going!*

Carlos only realised right at the last moment that I was actually going. As he got to his feet he tried to change his angle to get out of my way. In surf of this size, getting off the back of the wave is easier said than done once you're committed. As he turned his board, the water from the side of his rail sprayed back up into my face, just as I was getting to my feet and starting to work out my trajectory straight down the ever-steepening, freight-training abyss below me.

I couldn't see a thing as I got up. I was completely blinded, on probably the biggest, scariest wave and drop of my life. How's that for your worst-case scenario come true? At the same time, while trying to avoid Carlos, I had adjusted my rail to move away from him and just managed to catch the inside edge on a small bump in the face. To do this on the apex of probably the biggest wave of your life is not good; if I had fallen right then, I would have been in the worst possible spot and the outcome would have been horrendous and possibly life-ending.

I was blind, so I focused all my remaining senses and tried to hold it together. I called on all my experience and my survival instincts, and just managed to shift my weight inside and underneath me as the spray lifted from my face. My vision cleared just in time for me to regain my composure and balance and aim straight down. Now that I could see where I was going, I wanted to close my eyes: I was staring down a 60-foot, sheer vertical drop, straight down, with a frightening wall up ahead.

Imagine being on top of a four-storey building that's travelling at 50 kilometres an hour, looking straight down and deciding that you're going to jump, on purpose! Well, now that I was in, I was committed. There was no turning back. I started dropping 10, 20, 30 feet as the wave got more and more vertical. Then, something you really don't want to have happen on a wave that size, happened – it went beyond vertical.

I started to feel weightless and like I was disconnecting from my board. The chances of making a weightless drop and reconnecting on a wave of this size and magnitude are very slim; the bigger the wave, the smaller your chances.

But just as I thought my front foot was going to disconnect, it let me down and I got to the bottom. I could see and hear the lip chasing me down, at high speed, and the bump on the smooth wave face was making it difficult to control the board chattering

under my feet. But I knew I had made the drop and was going to survive. As soon as I got down to the bottom I looked up and went super low and wide into my bottom turn; I could see a big section up ahead that I wasn't sure I could make, so I drove as hard off the bottom as I could to keep my speed and get as high as physically possible.

It dawned on me then: this whole section was about to fold out and over. I could try to go down and outrun it before it smashed me, which at this point seemed inevitable, or I could do what few dare to do and what I had always dreamt of doing at Mavericks: I could pull up into it, into the biggest grinding cathedral barrel of my life. It isn't a prospect for the fainthearted. It's a scary place to be and it's hard to get into that position. Once you commit, there's no turning back. The only escape route is through the eye of the storm – or, more precisely, the eye of the barrel.

I saw my chance and I didn't hesitate. I just took it. I was all in, no matter what.

I drew up even higher, put my hand in the face of the wave to further stabilise myself and then trimmed along the belly of the beast, just waiting for her to swallow me whole. That's when her scary shadow descended and she engulfed me.

I was travelling inside this massive, spinning tunnel of water. It was perfect, it was magical, it was everything I had ever dreamt of and more. I was riding inside a barrel at the Mavericks Big Wave Invitational, as one of the top 24 big-wave surfers in the world, with 60 000 spectators watching from the cliffs, another 80 000 watching live from the AT&T Park in San Francisco on two 80-metre Jumbotrons, and over two million, including my friends and family back home, watching in their living rooms around the world. I was in heaven.

In that second it dawned on me that if I could get this far, if I could pull into a barrel like this on one of the biggest waves I'd ever surfed, on the heels of a near-death experience, if I was really smart, if I survived this and played the game and got into the final, I could actually win this thing. I could win the Mavericks Invitational on the biggest day in the event's history.

Through the eye of the barrel, I watched the spectator and judges' boats go past. As the eye got smaller and smaller, I knew it wasn't going to let me out. This monster was going to eat me alive after all. As the foam ball inside the wave engulfed me, I jumped forwards over the front of my board, praying that the beating I was about to endure wasn't going to be too severe and it would let me out in one piece.

And then the tumbling started, and with it the powerlessness of knowing there's nothing you can do but try to go with it as much as you can and hope it lets you up before you black out and run out of air. I rolled and rolled until I had to breathe, and then I started swimming. I surfaced more quickly than I expected. As I popped up, the rescue ski was there within seconds; he grabbed me and took me back into the channel.

Whoohoo, that was awesome! The most insane thing ever! Yeehah, I did it! I had survived the wave and the heat was seconds away from winding down. I knew I had to be through into the final on those two waves. I was so stoked and pumped. Everyone was hooting and cheering from the boats. That was one of the best waves of my life, for sure. I was just tripping on the adrenaline, buzzing and beaming, and then I got the results: I was second and through to the final of the Mavericks Big Wave Invitational.

Everything I had ever dreamt of had come true.

Well, almost everything ...

The final

It was now late in the afternoon. I was starting to cramp all over from the fatigue, exhaustion and lack of sleep. Adrenaline can only take you so far, and the 42-hour trip was starting to catch up with

me. I'd been sitting in my wetsuit all day and I was cold; the sky had become overcast and the swell was looking even more ragged, rugged and menacing than ever. It had been building all day and it was finally peaking, with the bigger waves reaching the 60- to 65-foot range – that's more than 20 to 22 metres high.

But I just had to suck it up and get my head right once more. This was the most important hour of my life. I knew that if my mind wasn't right, I shouldn't be going out there at all; it would be plain stupidity and possibly suicidal.

I needed to get amped, warm, focused and energised – quickly. I had two more Clif glucose shots, two bananas and lots of water, and started doing some exercises to get warm and loosen up, while at the same time keeping a close eye on the clock and the ocean.

The more I watched, the more nervous I became. As the sky clouded over and the wind started to build, the waves detonating all over the reef seemed even bigger.

There were six of us in the final: Dave Wassel, Anthony Tashnick, Carlos Burle, Shane Desmond, Skinny Collins and me. The officials started handing out the vests. I put mine on and turned to the other guys to wish them luck. Especially Carlos – I gave him a big hug and said, "It's a privilege and an honour to be surfing out here with you in the final, brother. Let's be safe, charge hard, and ensure that we both make it back in one piece!"

Then we headed out to the back line. I sat on my board, splashed some of that cold Pacific Ocean on my face, closed my eyes, breathed in, held it there, focused on everything I needed to do, and then slowly let it all go.

Clean the slate, push the reset button, let go of any negative or limiting thoughts, focus. You can do this!

This was my day, my time, everything I'd been working towards: right here, right now, right in front of me. *So what are you going to do with it?* I asked myself.

I looked down at my board, at the names of all the people

back home who had never stopped believing in me, my passion, my determination and my ability to win this event and do South Africa proud.

I thought of my dad and knew he would be proud of me. I wondered what he would say to me at that moment. And then I looked down at my board again and saw that one sticker in the centre of the deck: "Chris would go!"

I smiled and said under my breath, "Yes, he would!" Then I lay down on my board and started paddling back out into the line-up.

No matter the outcome, I was here. I was in the final. I was going to try to play it smart, cool, calm and collected – if that was even possible. It had never been my way or my strategy, but today was different. This wasn't any normal day – this was the day of days; a day for rewriting surfing history; a day for the brave, the clever, the calculating, the cunning and the courageous.

A lot had changed since coming out of the semis 90 minutes ago, when I was all pumped and thought I could win; physically I was weaker and more fatigued, and while my mental state had improved, the elements had not. The already enormous waves had become trickier in every sense; the wind had picked up and the tide had dropped out further, making the waves even steeper, gnarlier and more dangerous. They were not only far bigger than they had been earlier in the day, but far bigger than anything anyone had ever attempted to paddle into.

Until now. I was about to go in, just hours after my worst near-death experience, with little to no sleep, on borrowed, backup equipment and in complete financial ruin. How's that for incentive? But none of that seemed to matter at all right then.

My strategy was simple: try to get a smaller wave right at the beginning of the heat, just as a starter, to relieve the pressure. Many of the competitors who had dropped out of the previous heats

had battled to get two waves in the allocated 45 minutes, so I needed to get one under my belt right at the beginning, then build on that with a mid-range one and, if I was in the right place and could find a big one with that "magic in", I would try to take it on and tame it before the end of the heat.

If I could manage all that, great; if not, so be it. Either way, that was my strategy. I would give it my best shot and try to stay alive. That was it.

As I got out into the back line, I hooted "Wooohorah" just as the contest horn sounded. "Let's do this, we're game on!" The final had begun.

As I started to move across, I realised there was going to be a pretty big set within the first three minutes, which is very unusual. I stroked over the first one. I was a little deeper than everyone else, but two of the guys were further out and that's when I saw the next one already capping. Was I too deep? And then the top of the wave, just six to eight feet of it, capped and broke, which instantly put the other two competitors off and they pulled out.

The wave looked somehow different in the way it broke, like it was moving and surging into a bigger lump of water in front of it. On any normal day, I wouldn't have even looked at this kind of wave, but this was no ordinary day. On a day like this you had to react to opportunities and be flexible. By now the face of the wave had a huge double lump in it, like two waves were merging. It looked really strange and ominous. In a split second, I decided I could maybe catch the corner of the broken part of the wave.

If I timed it right, it could slingshot me into the main part of the wave, before or as it doubled up, and then lurch and throw out properly over the main bowl before it got to the inside shelf. I spun around and paddled with everything I had. The white water from the broken corner clipped me, just enough to push me in, but not enough to throw me off. I was on. I quickly got to my feet. This was good, but as I came out of the corner of the white water I realised I was surfing down an eight-foot wave, onto the top of a 50-foot wave that was just capping and about to lurch out into something quite evil and scary when it hit the main reef. I was riding just the top bit, but the wave was mutating and merging into the bigger wave in front of it.

But I was in. I was riding the first wave in the first two minutes of the final. It was everything I had wished for! But as I rode up on the crest of that huge wave, I knew that something was slightly off. I could go over that ledge and possibly make the biggest, heaviest drop of my life, and maybe even pull into the barrel as it doubled up and lurched out. But it was doubling up dangerously and way too quickly; if I went over the ledge and committed to this drop and got it wrong, or if it went too steep and vertical quicker than I anticipated, there would be no escape and that would be the end of my heat, my day and possibly my life.

Normally I wouldn't have flinched; I would have just gone. But on this day, mistakes could be fatal and it was just too early in the final to risk it all. The odds just didn't look like they were in my favour – in fact, they looked heavily stacked against me – even though, now that I was up and riding, every fibre in my body and mind was screaming, "Goooooooo!"

All this rationalising, this life-or-death decision-making, hap-pened in the split second I was teetering on the brink, hanging on the edge while I rode along the top line of that cresting lip, looking over the edge of this heaving, gurgling, warping monster. I looked down over the ledge of the massive wave, seesawing between going and not going. It was a decision that could change my life forever. Or end it.

Suddenly I thought: *It's too early in the heat to do this; there is too much at stake.* At the absolute last second, I slid off the back

and out the other side. I got back onto my board, put my head down and started scratching for the horizon, because now I was 50 metres inside of everyone else. I wasn't in a good place and didn't want to get caught inside either.

It was the first time in my life that I had ever pulled out of that kind of wave once I had committed and got to my feet. I never pull out of waves. I'd rather go down in flames knowing that I tried than pull out. But there was just something about that wave that didn't seem right, and it was too early in the heat to take such a big risk. Yet I was cursing myself in my head; I couldn't believe what I had just done, but I knew deep down inside that it was probably the right decision.

What I didn't know was that back home, where my friends and family were watching live on the internet, both my brothers and all my friends were screaming at me to pull out of the wave. Because what I couldn't see, they could: the bump in the wave where it had doubled up was ginormous. If I'd gone over the ledge and dropped back into the next part of the main wave as it grew, it would've stood up too quickly, lurched out and completely obliterated me. Without a doubt it would have killed me.

Pulling out of that wave was one the hardest decisions I've ever had to make, but it turned out to be the best decision of my life.

It was another 10 minutes or so before the next set came in fast and furious. I was slightly out of position for this one, and instead of risking getting hammered, I played it smart and conserved my energy. Still, it was frustrating to watch three of the other guys catch waves in that set. I paddled further across, hoping to be in a better spot for what came next. But it was a mind game out there, as the playing field had got exponentially bigger and the waves even wilder, scarier and more out of control. They were now breaking and moving all over the impact zone.

I realised that, after everything was done and the event was over, there would be no looking back and making excuses. It was the same out there for all of us. We were all scared; we were all out of our comfort zone. Today was about who was going to be the smartest, who was going to play the game wisely, get two massive waves and survive it all. It was about the true essence of a waterman: which athlete could adapt to the volatile and changing playing field, be flexible, make it work and come out unscathed in an environment that was so frightening it was simply unfathomable. It was about more than athleticism; it had to do with courage, heart, determination, commitment, endurance and sacrifice.

I waited patiently, observing everything and constantly adjusting to the movement around me: the wind, the currents, the tide and rips, the turbulence of the breaking waves – everything was constantly changing.

As the tide turned, the playing field shifted to the right. I started moving left as I saw something coming on the horizon. Only two other competitors were out at the back, so I had room to play the field without getting jostled for position and pushed too deep.

Paddling over the first wave, I started taking slow, deep breaths to get more oxygen into my system in preparation for what was to come. As I came over the first, the second loomed. I was too deep. Shit! The second wave was already bigger than I thought. I dug deep and quickened my stroke; I would just make it over this one if I gave it everything – *Go, go, go!*

It rose 40, 50, 60 feet, as I paddled up the face. At the last second I broke the crest and punched my way over the top. I heard it heaving, sucking and exploding behind me, drawing all the water and trying to pull me back over with it. I had made it, but my heart was in my mouth; that was way too close for comfort.

The spray cleared while I frantically paddled out, but the third wave was already there, waiting to jump on me. Just as I paddled for

the shoulder, I saw that Skinny was too deep; he bailed his board over the top and, at the last second, the wave seemed to hold back and slow down, as if it was breathing in before unloading everything it had on the reef below. I was just far enough across now – not right on the apex but fractionally on the side of that peak – to be momentarily in the right place. If I swung right now, right this instant, I could make it. Without a second thought, I pivoted, put my head down and put everything into stroking as hard as I could.

I dug deep and fast with my arms; I wanted this wave. I had to get it. I felt the wave regain its momentum, rear up and begin to lurch as I got to my feet. I pushed my weight forward and angled my board onto its edge so I didn't free-fall straight down into the pit; I knew I wouldn't make a 20-foot air drop. I just managed to hold the edge of my Clark in the face, and as it started getting vertical I grabbed the face with my hand to steady myself, even though this increased the chance of my board disconnecting. Luckily it just held.

As my board's nose reached the bottom of the pit of the wave, it looked like it was going to catch and nosedive, but I managed to quickly draw my weight back far enough to keep it from penetrating and myself from going over head first. I just managed to hang on for the critical drop, and crank straight into a deep and hard bottom turn, pull back up onto the face of the wave, straight up into the pocket and a nice, smooth 20-foot arcing, wrapping turn all the way around into the white water.

Awesome, perfectly done, I thought to myself. *One down, Bertish, one to go.*

I had one solid wave under my belt. Now, if I wanted a good result, I needed another. But not just *any* wave; I needed the big one.

I looked down at my watch: with 4 minutes 50 seconds to go, there was time for one more set. Since we'd only had one really big set in the first 10 minutes, theoretically we were due another one soon. Would it come before the end of the heat and would I be in position? More importantly, would I have the courage and balls to spin and go? I was about to find out, because, when I looked up again, I saw it.

A massive bump on the horizon had started to form and was getting bigger with every second. Everyone on the boats was whistling and going berserk. They knew this was the last big set of the event, and all of us competitors were out there waiting for it, all jostling around, trying however we could to ensure that we were in the perfect place for it.

Anthony Tashnick was at the back, 30 metres further out than the rest of us, hoping for a roll-in on one of the bigger ones. Skinny was 30 metres on the inside, waiting for the medium ones that would slip under most of us. And then there were Carlos and me, the deepest, right next to each other. Skinny Collins was 10 metres wider and slightly further in, hoping we weren't going to catch it, so he could get it. And Shane Desmond was 20 metres to our left, sitting wider, not wanting to get caught too deep.

As I saw the first monster building, I knew it was going to be a really good one. It was thick and massive and coming in from deep. Was it going to peak on the outside ledge and let Tazzy in, as he turned to try to get it 30 metres out? It could break. He paddled …

I tried with all my might to hold my ground – easier said than done when the wave looks like it's going to stand up into an over-60-foot-high wall of water and is moving towards you at high speed and could break on your head. Every part of me was telling me to paddle for the horizon, but I knew if I could just hold my ground, I might be in the right spot to catch this monster – as long as Tazzy didn't get it first.

Tazzy paddled, but was just too far out to catch it. It seemed to hold back on the outside ledge, just enough to not break. But now

it was bearing down on Carlos and me. As it got closer it started peaking and frothing at the top like some angry beast. Carlos was five to 10 feet outside of me and I saw him out of the corner of my eye starting to turn and paddle. I knew instantly that he was going to go. I have looked up to Carlos most of my big-wave life and I knew that once he paddled for a wave, he was committed.

I looked down at my board for an instant, just long enough to catch a glimpse of something special, something that was there for a reason, for this exact moment. One line: "Chris would go!"

Everything flashed through my brain in that split second. Everything that had happened to get me to this point. This was the goal I had been chasing for 10 years. This was the exact moment. I needed to seize this opportunity with zero hesitation and fear, and 100 per cent commitment. Live, die, fall, falter or ride to glory, the time was now. This was it!

I put on the brakes, leant back, swivelled my board and aimed just to the inside. I was already 10 feet inside of Carlos; this would give me the inside track and right of way, since I was also further out than him. I could feel the wave standing up and starting to cap behind me. *Please don't let it break over me*, I thought, *I'll be so screwed.*

To be pushed over the falls on the first wave of the set, with others following, ready to run me down – that would be the worst-case scenario. That's why you don't generally go for the first wave in the set ...

No ... delete any negative thoughts, focus on the positive outcome. I put everything into those few key strokes, literally everything! I was all in.

And then a strange thing happened: the wave began to look like the one I had visualised in my mind before I went to sleep the night before. Could it really be happening again, like it had at Jaws?

I just squeaked past Carlos as the wave started to lift and carry me. As I got to my feet, the top was capping and breaking right beside me, but I was on. I was just in on the corner of it, right up at the top, but as I got to my feet I knew there was a big ledge ahead. I could see that I was going to have to ride over it and then still try to make the drop, before it doubled up and started lurching out. And then I saw the gap, like a little ramp, to get in and over the ledge. It was the moment of truth. I had to take it – it was now or never.

As I dropped in over the ledge, I saw it: that big bump mid-face of the wave, which I had seen in my dream. It was staring right at me and I knew I was going to hit it and go airborne, which is what you don't want when you're travelling at speed on a wave of this size and magnitude. Everything would depend on how I got through this. If I stiffened, I would probably fall after launching over it. I needed to do it exactly as I had visualised it the night before: stay nimble, loose and flexible, be Elastoman, flow with it, unlock and unhinge, collect myself and regain balance at the bottom – *if* I made it to the bottom without falling.

I hit it and it knocked me slightly off-balance as my board disconnected from the wave face for an instant. I was purposefully low and coiled up like a spring when I hit it, so that when I started to go off-balance and disconnect I could respond by unravelling. I went into full stretch to absorb the free-fall drop. My toes were only just touching the board, trying to maintain control, but my body was way off-centre. As I reconnected with my board, I tried to use my feet to bring it in under me.

I knew I would struggle to keep it together – I was now dropping down a massive precipice, 30, 40, 50 feet. I centred myself above my board and started compressing my body. My head was pulling to the side and I knew I was in trouble. As I felt myself starting to fall, I stuck out my hand and grabbed the side of the wave. It was just enough to stop me from going headfirst over

the side. I managed to regain my composure and balance, and looked up as I hit the bottom of the wave.

The huge monster was about to come down on me. I knew I had to get my board on a rail quickly, to make it around the detonation of the lip. I pushed down hard with everything I had on that inside rail and drew a long, low and hard turn off the bottom. I looked up again to see what seemed like the entire ocean bearing down like an avalanche towards me. I knew I wasn't going to make it around this section. I was going to try to straighten out and outrun it, but I knew what the result was going to be. I had made the most critical part of the wave, but I was going to get run down and smashed by the thundering white water. I couldn't avoid it; it was inevitable. I just needed to survive this one last obstacle and then I could go home.

Here we go, brace, deep breath, relax, you can get through this.

Then the thundering lip exploded right on the back of my board, throwing me up into the air as if I were diving off a springboard. As I made impact with the water, I realised it was only just about to begin, again!

That wave hit me from behind so hard and with such immense force that it pushed my teeth right through the bottom of my mouth. That was before the turbulence gripped me underwater and shook me so violently that it felt as if it was trying to tear me apart.

Getting to the surface now became the most important thing, just getting to where I could take one crucial breath. Somehow I managed to get my head above the foam. I could see the rescue-ski operator trying to get to me, but the turbulence was too great.

Then I was back under, held down for what seemed like ages. When it let me go I clawed to get up to the surface for a breath. Then the next one was on me, then the next. Two waves, three waves passed. I knew I wouldn't be able to keep this up for much longer.

Then the rescue ski was there, flying in quickly to pluck me up and onto the sled. We headed out of the danger zone at pace and into the channel, to safety.

The buzzer sounded for the end of the final. It was over. I had survived. I had conquered my fears. I had achieved everything I had set out to achieve. I had faced the mighty monsters of the deep, the real Titans of Mavericks, and survived.

It took me at least 20 minutes to paddle back to the beach. I'm still not sure why I didn't get a ride in on one of the skis. Maybe I just wanted to be in the moment, to reflect, to savour the blissful realisation that I was still alive and had survived it all – not only the waves, but everything that had gone into the last 60 hours. It had been epic, in every way.

By the time I reached the beach, I was so exhausted I didn't really know what was going on. I walked about 50 metres up the beach and was mobbed by journalists and photographers. More and more people kept crowding around. I couldn't process every-thing. I assumed all of the other surfers were being interviewed, too. Everyone kept asking me how I felt.

"I feel exhausted, just relieved to be on land and happy to be alive. It feels great. I'm just honoured to have competed here today, on the Day of Days, with all these legends and heroes of mine. I think I did okay. To be back on dry land after surviving a day like that is huge in itself!"

They asked me the same questions, over and over. But no one thought to tell me the actual result. Until my friend Ryan Seelbach, who had been surfing in the event, came up behind me and grabbed me by the shoulder.

"Chris, what are you talking about? Stop being so humble man, you've won! You've just won the frikkin' Mavericks Big Wave Invitational on the biggest day ever!"

They'd announced it on the beach while I was still trying to get back in.

I looked up and saw all the other big-wave surfers standing around. Some were being interviewed, but none of them were surrounded by hundreds of reporters like I was. That's when it actually hit me. Holy shit! I'd won! I'd actually won the Mavericks Invitational!

I raised my hands above my head and someone poured a beer over me. It was real! And the celebrations had just begun!

Normally I would have been put up on a podium and handed the award right then and there, but the podium and the speakers and the PA system had been washed away into the lagoon. None of it mattered, though. What mattered was that my dream had come true. All the hard work, the risks, the sacrifices, the unwavering faith, the dogged determination to keep on going against all odds, to never give up, to never give in ... It had all finally come together on this one crazy, epic day, and it was all worth it, every last drop.

I stayed on the beach and signed posters, caps and shirts for fans for hours, and then again up at Jeff's Mavericks Surf Shop, until we ran out of ink and I couldn't use my hand any more. Then we all moved up to the Oceana Hotel for the ceremony and prize-giving. Those were probably the most memorable couple of hours of my life. When they handed over the winner's trophy and the $50 000 cheque, the whole room roared and I was lifted up onto the shoulders of giants, South African big-wave riders Mike Schlebach, Frank Solomon and Twiggy Baker, and my mentor, brother and amazing friend, Jeff Clark. It was such a special moment, one that I will remember forever. It was a testament to the fact that if you truly believe, have courage, stay focused and determined, work hard, never give up and never give in, dreams really can come true.

The festivities went on into the early hours of the following morning, and rightfully so ... It would come to be known as the

"Day of Days", the day that Mavericks thundered and roared, and the paddle-in surfers answered the call and came to do battle with the monsters of the deep. All 24 gladiators survived, a little battered and bruised and totally spent, but alive and able to tell the story of the day that changed the sport of big-wave surfing forever.

It was awesome to share that night with my big-wave brothers, my friends, the heroes and legends who had risked everything that day, not for money, but for the thrill, the love, the rush of riding those beasts, and living to ride another day. We were ecstatic beyond imagination. Although drained and fatigued, we were on an adrenaline high. We were STOKED, in every sense of the word!

Homecoming

Early the next morning, Jeff drove me to the airport. I had the clothes on my back, a trophy in my hand, a massive weight off my shoulders and a huge smile on my face.

Jeff is such a great friend and mentor. He's become like family over the years. If I hadn't met him all those years ago in that misty car park, my life would have been very different. I gave him a massive hug and said goodbye.

I was just about to board the plane when my phone rang in my pocket. It was the Mavericks event organiser, Keir Beadling.

"Chris! Congratulations again. Wow, what a massive achievement for yesterday. Listen, we've got this whole roadshow organised for you over the next week. We'll be flying you out to Las Vegas tomorrow, then LA, Miami, Washington, New York, and then back to the Bay Area for the finale in San Fran at the end of next week. We've got radio and television stations lined up ready to interview you—"

"Hold on," I interrupted. "Sorry, Keir, I did all the interviews yesterday. I'm at the airport, just about to get on a flight."

"What? What you doing there? Where are you going?"

"I'm flying home."

"But you can't go home."

"I have to, Keir. I don't think you understand. I work for a living. I've got a job to do and appointments booked for Monday morning."

He couldn't believe it. Surely I could change my plans? But I couldn't. I'd said I'd be back on Monday, so I was going to be there, no matter what.

I've never been one to admit how hard I've had it, but I've never had the luxury of being a professional surfer and getting paid to chase my dreams. I've had to pay for everything out of my own pocket, using my own – or borrowed – money. I've had the occasional sponsor – a couple of wetsuits and T-shirts here and there – but I've always had to pay my own way. And that's okay; at the end of the day, it made the victory even sweeter, to know how hard I had worked for it. I finished third in the world on the Big Wave Tour that year.

As I got to the boarding gate, the flight attendant took my boarding pass, swiped it, looked at me and then burst out, "Oh my God, you're that guy, the guy who won the Big Waves Mavericks event yesterday, aren't you? I saw you on NBC news last night – Chris Bertish?"

"Yes," I said. "I'm just happy to be going home alive, in one piece!"

"Well, on behalf of Virgin America, we're honoured to have you on the flight. Let me see if I can upgrade you."

And they did. When I walked onto the plane a couple of minutes later, an announcement came over the PA system: "This is the captain speaking. On behalf of Virgin America, I'd like to welcome a very special passenger on board today. Let's give a big round of applause to our 2010 Big Wave Champion from the monster waves out at Mavericks yesterday – we welcome Mr Chris Bertish on his way back to South Africa."

The entire plane erupted into hoots and applause. Wow, the impact I'd made in the event was just beginning to hit home. It was like winning the Super Bowl of surfing! In America, everyone was talking about it and it was all over the news – it was everywhere.

After travelling another 42 hours, I finally arrived at Cape Town International Airport. My brothers, ex-girlfriend, and a whole bunch of close friends and fans were waiting for me in the arrivals hall with banners and champagne. It was such a proud moment and an awesome surprise.

I stayed and celebrated with them for 15 minutes, did some quick interviews and then had to excuse myself. When I got back to my car, I placed my trophy on the seat next to me, changed into a fresh, smart shirt, paid for my parking – I laughed when I realised I could only just cover the R298 parking fee – and headed straight to my first Monday-morning appointment in Somerset West at 9:30 a.m. I managed to have a quick shave and brush my teeth at red traffic lights on the way.

I arrived at my meeting exactly 10 minutes late, and the client started giving me hell.

I considered telling her my whole story. The 10 years of hard work and sacrifice, the massive waves, the near-death experiences, the financial costs, the stress, the lack of sleep, the missed flights, the kindness of strangers. Waves the size of four-storey buildings. I thought about telling her all of it.

Instead, I just smiled and said, "Sorry, ma'am, I got stuck in traffic."

Epilogue

A new dream

I left that appointment and went straight to the next one, and the next one. I put in the usual 12-hour work day, because that's what I do when I'm not training or in the water.

As I've said, I don't get paid to surf. I had hoped that the $50 000 in prize money from the Mavericks Invitational would help me get out of my financial hole, but, as with most things in my life, it's never quite that simple.

After a legal battle between the contest organisers and sponsors, the company filed for bankruptcy, so I never got the full prize money due. But I did get exactly the amount I needed, almost to the cent, to pay back all the people I had borrowed from to get me to the event and to California that year and to settle all my credit cards and debts with the bank. I was left with zero. I was exactly back to square one.

And, actually, it felt just right. It was never about the money. There was nothing about making large amounts of money in the dream I had been working towards for so long. I just wanted to achieve a personal goal, one that I truly believed, with every fibre of my being, was possible, and then use that success to inspire others.

It all starts with believing in yourself. I believe in myself with 100 per cent conviction. I have an obsessive passion for living life to the full, for pushing as far as I can in everything I do. I like to squeeze the most out of life. I try to make every second count and do the things I love while I still can, before my body isn't able to do them any more. I never want to look back and think that I had the opportunity to do something and never took it. A life filled with regret is no life at all.

I remember a moment when I was flying over to defend my Mavericks Invitational title at the end of 2011. On the plane, I started thinking about the journey and how long it had been and how hard I had worked and how much I had sacrificed to get there, what I'd achieved and the friendships I'd made along the way.

I think it was the first time since winning the event that I'd actually had the time to stop and sit and think about it all. Life is made up of many important little moments, and you need to slow down sometimes, stop and appreciate them, enjoy the journey and what you have achieved along the way.

As I sat there on the plane, a wave of emotion came flooding over me. Tears started streaming down my face. I had dreamt about achieving my goals for so long. I remembered being 13 years old, sitting on my friend Anthony Kyle's carpet at his house in Kalk Bay, and watching surf movies. There was an insert about the Eddie Aikau Invitational (often just called the Eddie), and as I watched Brock Little dropping down into the biggest wave I had ever seen, I remember turning to Anthony and saying, "One day I'm going to ride the biggest waves in the world and pull into monster barrels like that!"

The thing is, I truly believed it. And here I was, 20 years later, travelling over to California and Hawaii to do just that.

When I started my journey, I had a love for surfing. But from that first big wave at Crayfish when I was just a teenager, riding big waves became a passion, and then an obsession. Once I'd achieved my goal of carving my name on the world's big waves, I felt like a weight had been lifted off my shoulders. I went full circle, back to just going out and riding big waves for the pure love, joy and stoke of the experience, for being in the ocean, for living in and appreciating the moment, before having to head back to shore and the chaos of daily life.

But of course it didn't all end there. Dreams don't end because they come true; some get ticked off and you move on, others evolve and grow. New goals emerge to take the place of the ones you've achieved. That's how you keep evolving and growing as a human being.

Since winning the Mavericks Invitational in 2010, I've also had to change. Everything I do will always involve water and the ocean. I needed a new challenge after ticking a couple of big ones off my list; I needed a new ocean-going sport to push my limits. I found it in stand-up paddleboarding. Supping combines all my water sports – wind-surfing, surfing and sailing – with a greater understanding of the ocean and the elements. It's the most versatile sport I know. I love that I can still catch big waves while supping, but at the same time use it to explore coastlines, rivers and water-falls, and even cross oceans between continents. (Watch this space!)

Over the last four years I've managed to learn so much from this new sport. It's taught me more about the ocean and the elements, as well as a great deal more about myself, my limits and my potential.

On my stand-up board I've managed to surf huge waves at Dungeons, Sunset, Crayfish Factory and Nelscott Reef. I've also been able to explore remote places, pioneer several day/night open-ocean adventures, follow and swim with almost every creature in the ocean, and set a couple of world records, including the first-ever unsupported solo paddle over 325 kilometres, and

a new Open Ocean Guinness World Record of 12 hours on a stand-up paddleboard (covering over 130 kilometres).

But I always want to push it further, naturally. One day I was chatting with some of my mates.

"What if you could use only the strength in your arms and all the skills across all the sports you've learnt over the years as a waterman to paddle all the way across the ocean, from one continent to another?" I asked them.

"That's impossible," they said.

"Is it?" I said, smiling.

Ready, steady, stoked!
What it takes to be a big-wave champion

Dream it/See it/Believe it/Achieve it. By now you know that this is my mantra, the code I live and train by. Over the years many people have asked me to share the secrets of my success, to tell them how I managed to achieve the things I have.

To this day, I still use many of the principles my father taught me. I've just built on them and used the life lessons I've learnt along the way to help me grow and evolve. Each year I take time out to analyse myself and reflect on how I can change, what I've learnt and how I can improve. It's all about figuring out how to keep building on the foundation, about tweaking it constantly so that you can move ahead stronger, better, faster and, most important of all, wiser.

In this book I've talked about the principles that have guided me in undertaking some of my extreme big-wave adventures, and the life lessons that I've learnt along the way. I think it was while I was writing about my brothers that I started thinking about the number three. There's great strength in that number. Look at the way three legs give strength to a stool or tripod. Or how three corners hold a triangle, working together to make it stable and stronger. Or the triad of Bertish brothers; I know we each feel stronger when we know the other two are there, watching our backs.

So I've summarised my principles into three: READY (have the dream and vision); STEADY (prepare and stay focused on the task ahead); and GO (that's the stoked part). I call it my "Rule of Three". Ready, steady, go! Or, in my case: Ready, steady, stoked!

1. Ready | Dream it

It starts with the dream, the vision; that thing that lights the fire, the passion, within you; that excites you and gives you purpose. For me, that thing was big-wave surfing.

Your dreams are what inspire you to challenge yourself to go beyond your limits. The only decision you have to make, the only choice, is whether you have the heart to follow your dreams and the courage to make them happen.

A big part of dreaming is creative visualisation – and I'm not just saying that because a lot of my best visualisations happen when I am trying to get to sleep before a big event! It still amazes me that the first wave I caught at Jaws was an exact replica of the one I had visualised. The bump was even in the exact same place. When I faced the real thing, I got over it and through it because I was prepared for it. And in the process I made history.

The same thing happened at Mavericks. There have been many such moments in my life, where I have visualised waves or certain obstacles and seen myself overcoming them, and then gone on to do so in real life. By preparing myself mentally in this way, I'm ready for the physical challenge when it comes.

I've used visualisation to help me repair after injury, too; my "miraculous" knee recovery just before the Nelscott event is proof of the power of a determined mind.

I know that if you believe in something strongly enough, you CAN and WILL make it happen. But dedication to your dreams also means sacrifice. It's not an easy road to travel, so decide beforehand what sacrifices you're prepared to make in order to live or achieve your dreams.

Once you have your vision, you need to hold onto it all the way through the preparation and training stages. And that can be tough. There will be times when you're tempted to give up, especially when you hit obstacles and distractions. That's when you have to dig deep, stay focused and persevere.

Which is why it's so important to follow your heart and never, ever, give up on your dreams.

2. Steady | See it. Believe it

Once you've got your eye on the prize, it's time to prepare. Visualise it so clearly that you can see it, feel it, hear it and taste it. It has to be crystal clear, in every detail. Visualisation is so important!

Preparation, planning, training, determination and perseverance are the keys to success. I like to say that luck is what happens when preparation meets opportunity, and the harder you work, the luckier you'll get.

Do your research and get to know your environment. The principle of "know before you go" is especially true when you are in a new environment. My first experiences at Waimea and Shark Point taught me this. By the time I got to Cribbar, I had learnt the lesson well.

I put countless hours, days and years of dedication and determination into my focused training regime, no matter where I was or how I was feeling. No excuses! If I was somewhere without waves – like when I was skippering boats around the Caribbean – I found other ways to build the fitness I would need before meeting the really big waves. I used free-diving and my own specific training regime to help me expand my lung capacity and my ability to hold my breath for long periods of time and prepare myself mentally. That training saved my life.

Physical fitness breeds confidence, so train properly. There are no short cuts to gettting super fit. Take it seriously, whether you're in the pool, running, cross-training or in the surf. And don't neglect nutrition – you've got to put back in to get out, as I learnt the hard way. You need to train your mind, too. In my case, that meant learning to relax and calm my thoughts in difficult, and often life-threatening, situations.

I'm not being pessimistic when I advise people to prepare for the worst and hope for the best. You will encounter obstacles. But obstacles are nothing more than opportunities in disguise; we just need to be able to recognise them, be flexible, and be ready to overcome them.

Remember, pain is temporary, but the regret of quitting lasts forever. And you don't want to have to live a life filled with regret.

People find hundreds of reasons why they can't do something. All you need to do is find one reason why you can, then focus on that and take action to make it happen. Every decision we make in life is just a choice, a simple decision, so choose wisely.

Every one of us has the ability to be more than we believe. Once we realise and recognise this, success will follow. Discover the most powerful and magical tool in the world, which we all have within our grasp: the belief in "self".

Every success starts with one small step, so don't procrastinate. Start now.

What you believe, you achieve; what you don't, you won't.

3. Stoked! | Achieve it

You've done the dreaming, the planning and the preparation. Now comes the hardest part: facing the challenge in the moment without turning back, giving up or backing down.

Of course you will experience fear. But remember that fear is normal, natural; however, if you don't conquer your fears, they will end up conquering you. In fact, I always recommend running towards your fears; the things you fear most are the things you need to confront first. I guarantee that you'll find your courage there, waiting for you. Get comfortable with your fears, let them help you rather than hinder you. Our greatest growth often lies in our lowest moments, although it's hard to see at the time. That is when you truly get to know yourself and what you are made of.

Problems and obstacles will always arise. There will be times when you just have to suck it up and push straight through them. And keep pushing. If you keep trying to go around or avoid a problem in life, you will never gain the experience, the insight and the lessons it has to teach you, so that you never have to travel that road again. A problem avoided is like a boomerang – it will always come back. A problem tackled, no matter how big or small, becomes a problem solved and another great life lesson to help you move forward.

My dad liked to say, "In life you need to have the foresight to know where you are going, the hindsight to know where you have come from and the insight to know when you are going too far." That knowledge often comes down to instinct. Always trust your gut: your instincts are always spot on.

Seize every opportunity you can. Don't be scared to make mistakes; a mistake is only a mistake if you make it twice. And don't be a talker. It's a great way to procrastinate, but while the talkers are talking, the doers are already doing!

In life, when you have the choice, don't do what's easy, do what's right. Trust your gut on that one; you'll know it when you feel it. Even if you need a "Chris would go!" sticker on the front of your board to remind you. Believe in yourself. You've done the preparation. Now make it come true.

You have one life. Live it. Enjoy it. Be passionate about it. If it doesn't feel right, change it. Life is about choices and you are the captain of your own ship. Do what makes you happy, not only what pays the bills.

I hope my story has shown you that if you set your sights on a goal – no matter how big or small – if you work hard at it, if you stay focused and determined, if you are resilient and never give up, and if you truly believe, you can achieve anything.

My challenge to you is to delete the two words "Can't" and "Impossible" from your life, your world and your vocabulary and see how it changes your world. Then think of something you have always wanted to do, find just one reason why you "can" achieve your next big goal, and then go out and MAKE IT HAPPEN.

Dream it. See it. Believe it. Achieve it.

Nothing's impossible unless you believe it to be …

Keep surfing, keep smiling and stay forever STOKED!

208

The 16 golden rules of riding big surf with confidence

1. Plan and prepare for the worst, then give it 110 per cent and hope for the best. If you're not able to work out how you can get yourself out of a worst-case scenario, then you shouldn't be going out there in the first place.

2. Research, planning and preparation, coupled with determination, perseverance and a never-give-up attitude, are key to big-wave success.

3. Physical fitness breeds confidence, so train very specifically for worst-case scenarios, so that you can handle them and are prepared if and when they happen.

4. When you paddle out, watch and wait – be patient. You need to see and be aware of what's happening in your environment. Get comfortable before you get into the thick of it.

5. Never paddle for the first wave of the set, because if you don't catch it or you fall, you will be in the worst possible place (the impact zone) for the next two to five waves.

6. Know yourself and your own personal limits and boundaries. Ultimately the only person you can rely on in big surf is yourself. So don't put yourself in a situation you are not able to handle and never rely on other people to be there to bail you out of trouble.

7. Test yourself constantly, to keep evolving, to keep getting better and stronger, and to help you shift and push your own comfort zone.

8. The most powerful tool in the world is an unwavering belief in oneself. Believing in yourself 100 per cent is everything.

9. Know and trust your equipment. Ensure you have the right tools/boards for the right waves. Foam is your friend – bigger boards with the right rocker help you catch waves. You have to be able to catch them first in order to get better. The right

board is key in big surf. Conversely, the wrong board can get you killed.

10. When you see that you are going to get caught inside, take a few big, deep breaths, and slow your breathing and paddling. Don't panic, calm your mind, relax, don't dive too deep, just go with the flow, don't fight it. Stressing and fighting use extra oxygen you don't have.

11. You have to really want it, so stay focused, put in the time and preparation, and persevere daily.

12. When you panic, don't panic! In the ocean, things are volatile and constantly changing, so the key is to stay calm and be flexible in order to change with it. Staying calm in intense, life-threatening situations can mean the difference between life and death.

13. Manage your fears so that they can help you rather than hinder you. Courage is not the absence of fear, just the ability to manage it and push through it. Remember that if not managed correctly, fear causes doubt, doubt causes hesitation, and hesitation will cause your worst nightmares to become reality.

14. No matter how bad things get, remember that it will be over within 30 seconds. All you are doing is managing an uncomfortable mental and physical state for a limited period of time.

15. Use the power of visualisation. See yourself making the waves, making the drops. If you fall, keep playing the movie over and over in your mind until you get it right. When you are paddling for a wave, you should be able to see yourself pulling out at the end of riding it, before you even get to your feet!

16. When you're paddling into a bigger wave and you think you're in, always take two extra strokes before you get to your feet. You'll always be glad that you did. And under no circumstances should you ever hesitate – once you commit, you go!

The right attitude and preparation is everything in big surf, like it is in life, so be bold, be brave, be confident, be respectful, be friendly, be humble at all times. The big-wave brotherhood is a very special group of individuals and we look out for one another at all times. It's a beautiful, humbling place to be, out there in the ocean when the sea is big and alive, and it's our job and duty to ensure we've got one another's back, to ensure we all come in safe, every one of us, at the end of each and every magical session. The ocean is my sanctuary, my teacher, my meditation, my happy place, my therapy, my church, my cathedral, my friend and the one place … I call home.

Thank you for helping me live another dream. By buying and reading this book, by enjoying it and feeling the stoke, by being inspired and sharing the passion, you are helping me fulfil my "why", which is helping to inspire others the world over.

To follow my latest big projects and adventures, or book me as a speaker at your next conference/event/function, go to: www.chrisbertish.com or follow me on Twitter @Chris_Bertish.

Acknowledgements

I would like to thank my mom, Fran, for staying strong through so much over the years. It hasn't been easy having three sons, especially after my dad passed away. Thank you for putting up with all the crazy stuff we've been up to for the past 40 years; it's meant the world to us, even if we never really mention it. Thank you.

To my incredible brothers, Conn and Greg, the other parts of my strength; you are my guides, my friends, my sages. Thanks for always being there for me, through thick and thin. I wouldn't be who I am today or have achieved what I have if it wasn't for you guys. The bond of the Bertish brothers has always been so strong, connected and woven together by the memory of Keith.

To my amazing, special and supportive wife, Clellind Bertish: thank you for your patience and understanding and for accepting me for who I am, my passion for adventure and supporting what I do. I love you.

To all my friends and former girlfriends who have helped me along the way, and who have shared special times, moments and memories with me, from Ange' and Linnelle to Lin, Tashi and Michaela. Thank you.

To all my friends who have stuck with me over the years: Dougie Boyes, Steve Hurt, Greg Casey, Carl Warburg, Ant Kyle,

Chris Devenish, Duncan Duvenager, Greg Brunt, Andrew and Linnelle Hoeks, the Jenkinsons, Rossiter, the Bradleys, Pauli and Lu Copson, Nic Blignaut, Graeme Carr, Paris Basson, Kerry McCullagh, Matt Marks, Ben Grenata, Darren Robertson, Rob Thomson, Ross McInnes and Lindsey Wilson.

To Craig and Carol Middleton, and Tess and Richard Streletski, from the Caribbean: we worked on the boats and raced together and are still such special friends.

To Jeff Clark, who has become like family, a brother, but who is also a mentor and an amazing friend: thanks for all your guidance and friendship over the past 15 years, since that very first chilly, misty evening we met in the Mavericks car park in 2001, when you took me in. Thanks for the incredible boards-magic flying peaches, and for being able to share so many magic sessions and memories with me all over the world. You are pure inspiration. And Cassie, thanks for all your love and support with Pico: you are the best.

To all the old-school surfers, the pioneers in Cape Town who showed me the way, especially Mikey Duffis, thanks for the inspiration. To Tich Paul, Johnny Paarman, Pierre DeVilliers, Pierre Doep, Glen Bee, Rosco Lindsey, Ian Armstrong and Cass Collier.

To the present guys who always support and push me and have helped shape me into a better surfer: my brothers, Mike Schlebach, James Taylor, Andy Marr, Simon Louwe, Jake, Barry Futter, Jacque Theron, Davey Smithers, Jack Smith, Jason Hayes, Frank Soloman, Doogle, Grant Baker, Jeremy Johnson, Roddi Torr, Seth, Rick Wall, and all the new young crew, like James Louwe, Phillip Nell, Josh Redman and Matt Bromley. Keep smiling, keep charging and chasing those swells, keep stoking your passion, and keep pushing your limits and boundaries. It's been an honour, a privilege and a pleasure charging waves with you all … when I'm out there at Sunset and the Factory, I'm home!

To all the surfers I have met along the way: we've shared some great times and some special waves and made some beautiful memories. Thank you.

The California and Hawaii crew: Dev Gregory, Tom Burlow, Greg and Rusty Long, Gary Linden, Mark Healey, Dorian, Kelly Slater, RCJ-Rosco, Carlos Burle, The Jackal, Clark Abbey, Ryan Seelbach, Jay Bird, Randy, Washie, Alex Martins, Skinny Collins, Sponsor, Curt, Eric-Powerlines, Frank Quirarte, Don Montgomery, Richard Hallman, Jason Murray, Rick Leeks, Seth Migdal, Bryan Overfelt-StarBar, Don Curry, Kelly Clark, Heiday and all the guys – you were always so welcoming and generous with your waves and your friendship, I really appreciate it.

And last but definitely not least, Tim Noakes, Lewis Pugh and Jacqui L'Ange, who guided me through the process of putting this book together: without your enormous help, this book wouldn't be what it is, so thank you, from the bottom of my heart.

Never forget to say thank you in life: it's important to show appreciation towards those who helped you on your journey, to all those who helped get you to where you are, so when you can, give a little back every chance you get, because every little bit helps and it often means a lot more than you may think to the person involved.

Thanks everyone for all the support. Keep dreaming big and then live with the courage to follow that dream.